shedding light on . . .

The
Dark Side
of Adoption

Marsha Riben

HARLO   DETROIT

Library of Congress Catalog Card No: 88-80003

ISBN: 0-8187-0105-6

Cover Illustration
by Barbara Axt
in memory of her son, Jim.

Harlo Press/50 Victor/Detroit, Michigan 48203

shedding light on . . .

The
Dark Side
of Adoption

Dedication

This book has been written in memory of Lisa Steinberg Launders, May 14, 1981 to November 4, 1987 and to all others for whom adoption has been a tragedy.

Contents

About the Author

MARSHA RIBEN is a former magazine editor and freelance writer who has written articles on the subject of adoption, parenting and childbirth for several national magazines. Mrs. Riben is a former lactation and childbirth educator, and the mother of four children, one of whom was lost to adoption in 1967. A member of Concerned United Birthparents, Adoption Triangle Ministry, A.L.A.R.M. and The American Adoption Congress, she has been an outspoken proponent of adoption reform since 1979. She is co-founder and former newsletter editor of ORIGINS, a New Jersey-based national organization for women who have lost children to adoption. She has appeared on two local TV networks and one local radio program speaking about adoption, has addressed the Health Education and Welfare Panel on The Model State Adoption Act, New York, as well as the New Jersey State Assembly Institutions, Health & Welfare Committee.

Acknowledgments

I wish to gratefully express my appreciation first and foremost to my husband, Todd, who believed in me even when I doubted myself. I wish to thank Adam, Matthew and Adira for their patience; Hilda and David Riben for their understanding and support; and Mary Anne Cohen, my mentor, my Doula, my guiding light and my inspiration.

I also with to thank Jone Carlson, Lynn Giddens, Carol Gustavson, Pat Johnston, Bobbi Moskowitz, Sandy Musser, Janet Osseroff, Pat Palmer, Mary Jo Rillera, Rachel Rivers and Joe Soll for their encouragement and Gail Davenport for bouncing ideas off.

This book is truly a labor of love. I am eternally grateful to those who believed in this project as much as I did and gave of themselves with no financial remuneration. People such as Barbara Axt, who illustrated the cover; Lucy Paré and Kathleen Eyerman for editing; Julie, Pat, Carol and Jerry Herman for their special contributions; and especially Carole Anderson and Pat de la Fuente for donating hours of editing and proofreading respectively. Your generosity helped to make this book a reality.

Finally I wish to thank anyone who is helped as a result of this book for justifying our combined efforts.

11

Introduction

The Foundation

But with each month that the babe within grows bigger the certainty grows stronger that her own destiny is intermingl'd with her child's. Henceforth, she shall define herself, at least in part, as the mother of that Babe. If it dyes, she is the mother of a dead Babe; if it lives, its Smiles and Tears will be her smiles and tears. If it is taken from her, still she is changed fore'er on Earth and in Heaven too. She has been doubl'd, then halv'd and she will ne'er be whole again. —Erica Jong, *Fanny*

In answer to the question, "Why this book?" I am reminded of a Holocaust survivor whose job had been to remove the dead bodies from the ovens. Just when he felt that he could take it no longer and was about to take his own life, a woman entering the gas chamber said to him: "You cannot die, for if there are no survivors there will be no one to testify." With no one to testify, the death of six million might have been denied to have happened at all, and worse yet, repeated.

I, too, am a survivor of tragedy. I am one of thousands

13

who survived the loss of our children to adoption and, while far less tragic than mass murder, they were, in many cases *not* "necessary losses." I have chosen to write about birth-parents' collective experiences, and to acknowledge all for whom adoption has been painful.

I wrote this book for the same reason I have been involved in adoption reform since 1979, for the same reason I co-founded ORIGINS, a national support organization for women who lost children to adoption. It is the same reason that Candy Lightner founded MADD (Mothers Against Drunk Driving)[2] and Gloria Yurkovitch founded Child Find.[3] Each of us became committed as a result of personal loss.

Does commitment mean obsession? Peggy Say, the sister of a hostage victim, uprooted her family to move to Washington, D.C. in order to help her brother and others. When she was asked if helping her brother had become an obsession, she answered, ". . . if by the word obsession, the definition is having this issue dominate every waking moment, then yes, it's an obsession. I don't like the term but it is probably reality. I see it in a different light. Many, many times during the day I'll find myself doing an everyday task and think of (him) . . ."

The Stephanie Roper Committee is another example of personal commitment. Founded by Stephanie Roper's mother after the brutal rape and murder of her barely twenty-two year old daughter, the committee has been called one of the most effective voices for victims' rights and has been responsible for the passage of three bills in Maryland.

People like Candy Lightner, Gloria Yurkovitch, Peggy Say and I have turned our obsessive, compulsive drive into positive energy because each of us has lost someone dear to us who is irreplaceable. Mrs. Roper said on "America Undercover" that victims do not seek revenge, but rather justice to be healed. Likewise birthmothers do not seek to reclaim, hurt or interfere. They merely seek reunification. Judith Viorst, in her book *Necessary Losses,*[4] wrote: "another defense against loss may be a compulsive need to take care of other people. Instead of aching, we help those who ache.''

With a limbo-loss there is no finality and no resolution, there is only coping and adjusting. There are many ways of coping with catastrophic loss. Mary Brachen Phillips wrote "Cradle Song," a play about losing her baby to Sudden Infant Death Syndrome. Ronda Slater wrote and performs a poignant one-woman play[5] about losing her child to adoption, her search and reunion. Bonnie Lee Black, who wrote the book *Somewhere Child*[6] about the abduction of her daughter by her estranged husband, once wrote in answer to a class assignment, "Why I Write," the following: ". . . I want to live a normal life, but find I can't. Someone shot me in the back of the soul and made me a cripple from here down. The dead legs dangle from the wheelchair, lifeless— see? I can no longer dance or make love. Only the hands of my heart can move. They move along the smooth paper, dragging a pencil, leaving a trail of jagged marks that spell: I AM STILL HERE.

"I am not a writer. I am a nothing, a no one, a meaningless being, barely alive, who's been blown halfway to nowhere, and has nowhere to go. I only write to prove that I was there." In a post script to her daughter, she further states, ". . . I have lived to write this story for you. For years I kept it locked inside, carrying it with me like a great weight, subconsciously waiting for the right time, when you'd be old enough to understand, when I'd be far enough away from the past to write about it without bitterness, hatred, or self-pity . . . I believe it is important for you to know the truth about your earliest years, because truth makes us free . . . For your sake I've tried to be strong. Professionally, I became a writer . . .''

In 1972, Frederick H. Stone of Glasgow, Scotland, recognized that in adoption "the three parties suffer loss: the mother who gives up her child, the child who fantasizes but will never know his real parents, and the adoptive parents who may unconsciously mourn the child they could not have themselves.''[7] I share the goal of Ronda Slater "to give birth-mothers validation for their feelings, to let adoptees know

15

that their birthparents do love them and to let adoptive parents know that we're not coming to steal our kids back.''

I write with no personal gain in mind; no hope of regaining my own lost child, or of regaining her love. Those are forever lost to me. I write with the hope of enlightening and educating many to the realities suffered by a substantial number of people whose lives have been permanently changed by adoption. I write to recognize adoption as an unfortunate necessity and to humanize the process. I cannot reverse my loss, but I seek to prevent future pain and offer an opportunity to those who consider adoption in their future to see it more realistically.

I write because someone must.

Part One

The Fantasies

"PREGNANT? MAKE A WINNING CHOICE . . . Choose The Adoption Option. Opt to Adopt and there will be three winners! YOU WIN peace of mind by giving your baby birth; YOUR BABY wins life and a chance for happiness; THE ADOPTING COUPLE wins a lovely baby to love and care for."
—*Brochure published by* Womanity, *2141 Young Valley Road, Walnut Creek, CA 94596.*

1

Dispelling
the Myths

"To be rooted is perhaps the most important and least recognized need of the human soul."—Simone Weil

"It would be nice if we could start by citing some current statistics about adoption" laments Lois Gilman, author of *The Adoption Resource Book,*[1] perhaps the most current and thorough book on the subject. But, she continues, such statistics simply do not exist. "The federal government has been out of the business of keeping track of adoptions for almost ten years now. We know how many hogs are in Illinois, but we don't know how many children are adopted. We have no idea of the total number of adoptions in the United States."

As if obtaining clear numbers of adoption placements weren't difficult enough, imagine the difficulties faced in trying to estimate the number of adoption disruptions. Agencies report a fifteen percent termination, or failure rate; one can only speculate what the figures would be if it included non-agency or private placements as well.

It is estimated that there are between five and nine million adopted persons in the United States today.[2] Taking the conservative figure and adding two adoptive parents and two birthparents for each adoptee there are twenty-five million people directly affected by adoption. This figure does not include four sets of grandparents (by adoption and by birth), siblings (by adoption and by birth), spouses, offspring, aunts, uncles, cousins, etc. At least half of the population, or 115 million people, are touched by adoption, excluding professionals, such as social workers and attorneys, who are actively involved in the process of adoption placement.

Thus, there are few people who do not at least know someone who is directly affected by adoption. They are either related to, or are themselves one of the parties in what has come to be known as the "adoption triangle"—adoptees, adoptive parents and birthparents.

Many of the people whose lives have been irrevocably changed by adoption have formed decided opinions about the process based solely on their own experience or perspective. These opinions, because they are so individual, are deeply rooted and emotionally based. For this reason, attacking some of these long-held beliefs is like attacking motherhood and apple pie. It may well be a hard, but necessary, pill for many to swallow.

After World War II many states introduced legislation which "sealed" adoption records, ostensibly to protect adopted people from the stigma of illegitimacy. Whether personally involved with adoption or not, we have all been exposed to a system shrouded with secrets. Where facts are destroyed, hidden and erased, only fantasy can remain. Where truth does not exist, lies are created. When honesty and openness are barred, secrecy and fear prevail. Because adoption as we know it in this country today is a system of secrecy, it is built on myths. Those personally involved have developed personal myths. Those who are not involved with adoption in any way have been exposed to terms such as "adoptees' rights," "birthparents' anonymity" and "search" through one form of the media or another. Even those whose only opinions about adoption are based on soap opera interpretations are reluctant to exchange fantasy for fact. Ask the average person who is not directly involved with adoption what he thinks of it and he will invariably

20

describe adoption in very positive terms. Most people see adoption as a way to find homes for homeless children and children for childless couples, while allowing young women to go on with their lives. Adoption is typically viewed as a solution to three problems. Margaret Mead noted in 1978, "Most Americans think adoption is a good thing."[3] Others, aware of the pain of infertility and the difficulties in adopting, build an image of adoptive parents as being noble.

The average uninvolved person has also formed opinions about the right to search. I once stood for several hours in a suburban shopping mall with a petition to open sealed adoption records in New Jersey. The majority of the people who passed by spoke of the birthmother's right to privacy and expressed fear that adoptees might find unpleasantness. They said things like: "It's better to leave the past in the past."

Pandora's Box needs to be opened, the skeletons must be let out of their closets, in the hope of shattering the many fantasies, myths, illusions, legends, fairy tales, assumptions and suppositions surrounding adoption. Most myths arise out of people's fear and ignorance to explain the inexplicable. What people do not understand they create myths to explain. More myths abound than reality where adoption is concerned because of the mystique surrounding the procedure.

MYTH: Adoption is a wonderful way of "matching" unwanted, homeless children with loving, waiting couples. The romanticized view of adoption is of loving couples who open their hearts and their homes to otherwise homeless orphans—the traditional "chosen child" story.

As in all fairy tales, the story ends with the assumption that they all live happily-ever-after. Attorneys and adoption agencies who place babies for adoption believe so firmly in this myth that most close the case once the adoption is finalized, feeling secure that the pre-placement screening is adequate to assure the future of the family. While in most cases their assumptions are realized, sadly, all too often this is not the case. Unfortunately, neither the "wonderful match" nor the "happily-ever-after" myth is always true.

FACT: Twenty years ago, there were abundant healthy white babies available for adoption. Today, the shortage of infants and toddlers available for agency adoption is so severe that the demand exceeds the supply by odds of over one hundred to one.

Today's teenage population is some six million smaller than that of the preceding generation. There are few people today, of any age, who would find it difficult to purchase one of many contraceptive devices which are sold over the counter. For those who experience an "untimely" pregnancy there are two options available today which were seldom available twenty years ago: legalized abortion and single parenthood.

At the same time that the pool of available white babies is drying up, an increase in infertility is being documented. Among married women in their early twenties, normally the most fertile age group, the incidence of infertility has jumped 117% between 1965 and 1982.[4] (More about the cause of this increase in Chapter Six.) Additionally, more couples are delaying marriage and parenting until their childbearing years are almost over. There is, therefore, a growing disparity between the number of infants surrendered for adoption and the number of couples seeking to adopt. Would-be adopters wait on agency lists for years for a chance at a healthy, white, newborn infant or seek other alternatives, such as artificial insemination by donor, surrogate mothering or embryo transplants. At the same time, these childless couples ignore the thousands of older, so-called "special needs" children who are free and clear for adoption but who do not meet their age, race or other physical requirements. These children remain in foster homes and institutions while couples compete for healthy, white newborn babies.

Despite media hype, such as an ad by The National Committee for Adoption which appeared in *Time* magazine and elsewhere in 1982, there are no homeless infants eagerly awaiting adoption.

22

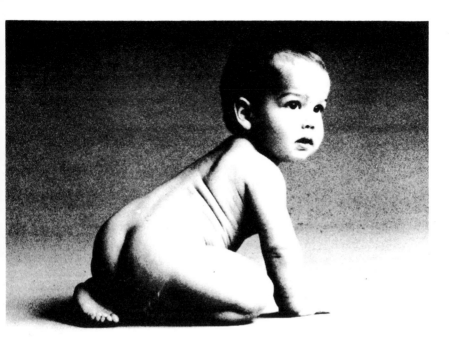

I Know My Baby Will Be Part of a Loving Family Because I'm Choosing Adoption

More and more teenagers with unplanned pregnancies are saying this. They know that making an adoption plan is a mature and positive way of showing their love for their child.

If you're pregnant and faced with decisions about possible solutions to your <u>problem,</u> call us in confidence. We'll give you the facts. You decide.

If you're calling about pregnancy, call collect. Call the National Adoption Hotline, (202) 463-7563.

National Committee for Adoption

Suite 326 · 1346 Connecticut Avenue, N.W.
Washington, D.C. 20036

Reprinted with the permission of the National Committee for Adoption, Inc., Suite 512, 2025 M St., N.W., Washington, D.C. 20036, Copyright 1982. (The underlining is the author's and did not appear in the ad.)

According to the 1982-83 Statistical Abstract of the United States from the Bureau of Census, unwanted births of all mothers 15 to 44, based on the National Survey of Family Growth in 1973, 13.1% of all births were categorized as "unwanted." In 1976 the number of "unwanted" births had decreased to 12.0%. In 1973, 84% of the women in the sampling were married and in 1976, 82% were married. The number of "unwanted" births did not increase as the marriage rate decreased, indicating that unmarried, unplanned and unwanted are not always synonymous.

As a result of responses received to the above mentioned ad, all subsequent materials produced by the National Committee eliminated the word "unwanted." William Pierce, President of the Committee, told me that "there is no such child who is 'unwanted' and I regret authorizing the use of that word."

The ad (See page 23) which replaces this one uses the word "problem" in regard to pregnancy. Will adopted persons feel any better about being described as a "problem" than they did about being told they were "unwanted?" (The underlinings of the word "unwanted" are mine and did not appear in the ad.)

If people who are as involved in adoption as the National Committee use wording which is insensitive to adoptees, is it any wonder that adoptees, adoptive parents and birthparents are subjected to cruel reminders every day?

A prime example of mass insensitivity was the Cabbage Patch "phenomenon" which persisted despite a warning by the American Academy of Child Psychiatry of the potential hazards of the doll to adopted children's understanding of their origins. In a November, 1983 letter to Arnold Greenberg, president of Coleco, the Academy wrote: "The doll arouses in children, especially adopted children, confusion, doubt and misunderstanding. They are receiving information contrary to information told by their parents, making the parents feel uncomfortable at best.

"The adoption 'gimmick' serves no worthwhile purpose in terms of recreation or education," continues the letter, "and the American Academy of Child Psychiatry hopes that you will withdraw the adoption aspect from its marketing. At the very least, it is not in good taste and is disturbing to many concerned with the health and happiness of children." While no one objects to the doll itself, many have shared the Academy's concern about the marketing techniques. In response to Cabbage Patch, Gloria Gruber of California, an attorney and adoptive mother, founded SPEAK, Society for the Protection and Education of Adopted Kids. Pam Hasegawa, New Jersey State Coordinator of Adoptees' Liberty Movement Association (ALMA), feels that what is wrong is "exploiting the 'if-it's-hard-to-get-it-must-be-valuable' mentality of most of the consuming world. We all know that adopting a baby is not easy these days."

Martin Brandfon, an adoptee, instituted a $100 million class action suit "on behalf of all adoptees, adoptive parents and birthparents who are offended and outraged at the exploitation of adoption in the ad marketing campaign of Coleco Industries." The suit claims that Coleco's campaign is "continuing to promulgate the misconceptions and misunderstandings about adoption that are prevalent among the non-adopted adults concerning the legal and social ramifications of adoption."

Cabbage Patch dolls, which are still being marketed, now including Koosas, Preemies, Twins and Travelers, are far from the only injustice that adopted persons must live with. There is an odd twist to the preconceived notions of adoption: while most people think of adoption in a positive way, adoption is often a "bad joke." For example, "You're so ugly, or so stupid, etc., you must have been adopted!"

In the motion picture *Volunteers,*[5] the father tells his problem son that he is adopted. "No, I'm not," the son protests. "I know," the father replies, "but please allow me that little fantasy."

Many adopted children begin their school experiences by proudly announcing that they are adopted, because it is often treated in their homes as something "special," and something to be proud of, only to learn very quickly that they are the focal point of teasing and jeering. Birthparents suffer from a similar inconsistency in attitudes. Prior to the birth of

their child they are told that surrender would be an unselfish act of love. Once they surrender, however, they become society's lepers.

In any other area of life, while such discrimination is likely to occur on a personal level, it would never be permitted publicly the way adoption discrimination is. Gail Davenport, M.S.W., A.C.S.W., Outreach Leader for Concerned United Birthparents and facilitator of the Birthparent Support Network, said of the Cabbage Patch dolls, "If any company were to introduce a black slave doll complete with transfer of ownership papers, we would see a public uproar because people are aware and sensitive to that issue. This is not the case with adoption . . ." Imagine "Black Dopes" for sale. Unconscionable, yet you can "Adopt-A-Dope" or Adopt A Pothole. DAK Industries, Inc.[6] runs a full page magazine advertisement with the headline "Illegitimate Child Adopted, now with new music vault housing!"

Imagine someone attempting to market a blind or handicapped doll that you wind up to have it fall down. Not very funny. And yet, our society quietly condones adoptees being the brunt of cruel and insensitive jokes such as the one portrayed on a nationally marketed greeting card which reads: "We thought this was the year to tell you . . . you're adopted!" and pictures "Dad" with his tongue out and "Mom" making an obscene gesture with her middle finger.[7]

Bob Cisco, supervisor of the Adolescent Unit of Rutgers Community Mental Health Center, sees a disproportionate number of adoptees in therapy. "Adoption," he says, "is a very loaded and sensitive issue for many people and we should make an effort to be aware and respect it. We should be cognizant of the cultural attitudes and values which we pass on to our children . . ."

Yet, rather than curtailing Madison Avenue hype, we are allowing it to pervade right into the heart of adoption. The Golden Cradle, an adoption agency which has received much publicity concerning its unique approach to adoption, places advertisements on billboards, fast food restaurant trays and in ladies rooms. What could possibly make an adopted person feel more like a commodity than to see such billboards

Adopt-a-pothole offered by town

BLACKFOOT, Idaho (AP) — Those lovable potholes that bring cars to their knees and send motorists through the roof are up for adoption in this Idaho town.

Under the program, residents can go to City Hall and identify potholes they wish to help repair. The adoption fee ranges from $5 to $25, depending on the size of the hole and its location.

The adoptive parents will be given a certificate noting the donation and the location of the pothole, which supposedly will receive loving attention from the street department.

and advertisements? Birthmothers seeing these glaring promotions are reminded of the pressures brought to bear upon them to make their difficult decision and often wonder if their children went to the best possible family, or merely to the family which could afford to pay agencies' high advertising costs.

The question that needs to be asked is: why do we need to promote adoption as an option to single mothers when there are thousands of homeless children awaiting placement? There is no doubt that adoption is best for children who will have two parents to love and care for them, assuming their birthparents do not. But there is no need to encourage family breakup merely to increase the available supply of babies to adopt. For unwanted, abandoned and orphaned children, adoption is preferable to long-term foster care or institutionalization, but in our haste to provide permanency we must not negate the equally important need of continuity. Every child needs and deserves both. Every adoptee deserves adoption to be made as humane as possible.

In 1978, Margaret Mead said that "our most basic beliefs about adoption—that children should 'match' their adoptive parents, that an adopted child should not know who her birthparents were, that foster parents may not adopt their foster children—are under attack from all sides. And now we must face the question, 'Where do we go from here'?"[8] Today, we still ask.

In his 1964 book, *Shared Fate,*[9] David Kirk argued that secrecy, deceit and failing to acknowledge the difference between families formed through birth and families formed through adoption put the long-term mental health of the children at risk. By the time his 1981 book, *Adoptive Kinship,*[10] was published, this idea was widely accepted in schools of social work throughout the country. Yet, in adoption *practice,* little has changed. In March, 1987 a New York State Appellate Court decision ruled against a 55-year-old adopted man's appeal for access to his birthfamily. In its decision, the court said, "The institution of adoption cannot survive without secrecy."

Henry Erlich, author of *A Time to Search,*[11] explains why changes of adoption practices have been slow in coming. "Sealed adoption records have impeded the correction of abuses by all kinds of adoption agencies, social workers, lawyers, and other independent adoption agencies. If law and social pressure had not prevented adoptees from investigating the circumstances of their own adoptions, the inadequacies of the system and the people who operate within it might have come to light long ago, and the publicity might have led to reform. Indeed, this secrecy doesn't guard anyone's rights as much as it hides the caprices of a generally uninformed class of people."

In order to begin to heal the wounds created by adoption, we must remove our rose-colored glasses and realistically evaluate the current adoption system before we promote it as a "winning choice." If it were really as ideal as some would have us believe, why then don't we take all children from their families of birth and place them with other families and thus have more "winners"? Just as reformers once fought to save the children who were being bought and sold as indentured servants by changing apprenticeship into adoption, so must those concerned with the welfare of adopted children work together to save the children who are victimized by the inadequacies of an outdated adoption system. We must begin by replacing myth with fact, difficult though that be.

A major publisher, in responding to an early draft of this book, wrote:

". . . the public will not buy a book with a negative point of view about adoption. Those who adopt do so out of necessity, not choice, and though they suspect abuses in the system, they are inclined to overlook the problems because they have no alternative. Seeing the subject realistically might be too painful and unacceptable."

I have too high a regard for my fellow men and women to believe that they would knowingly choose to overlook any abuse to children simply because it served their purposes. There are alternatives. As a society we have recognized that many children are subjected to unspeakable abuse in our day-care centers. We have responded to that knowledge by attempting to correct the flaws in those systems which allowed atrocities to take place. That same approach needs to be applied to the institution of adoption.

MYTH: Adoption provides children with two parents who will love them.

FACT: Many birthmothers love and want their children and only surrender because they are told it is the loving thing to do or because they fail to receive the help they need.

FACT: Although only two percent of the population is adopted, approximately twenty-five percent of those adolescents known to mental health facilities are adopted.[12] Most were adopted as infants. This is because adoptees often experience the surrender by their original mother as a rejection. This feeling of rejection often cannot be alleviated by even the most loving parents.[13]

FACT: Adoptions fail at a rate of at least fifteen percent.

FACT: Childless couples suffer pressure to conform to society's model of the ideal, nuclear family.

FACT: Adoptive parents are often ill-prepared for their children's natural curiosity regarding their heritage, and most operate in a void where their children's medical history is concerned.

MYTH: Adoption is best for the single mother who will forget and go on with her life.

FACT: Birthparents have been shown to experience lifelong grief as a result of the loss of their children.

ADOPTION: WHOSE CHILD IS IT ANYWAY?

A mother and a father and a mother. That's one parent too many: A tragic triangle, with all sides likely to be hurt.

More and more, young women who claim they were talked into giving up their babies are demanding legislation for open adoption records. In some cases, they're going underground to obtain information from legally sealed adoption records.

Consequently, adoptive parents live in dread at the thought of opening the door one day and finding their child's natural mother standing there. At the same time, adult adoptees searching for their roots are frustrated and angry because their past has been cut off.

Join Betty Furness for this 3-part investigation that reports on all sides of this tragic triangle and asks the difficult question: Whose child is it, anyway?

NEWS 4 NEW YORK
Starting tonight at 6.

Courtesy of WNBC-TV.

Because of the secrecy that birthparents are consigned to, they have been obscured, "shadowy figures,"[14] who have mainstreamed totally unbeknownst to anyone. The nice lady next door with all the kids, the president of your bank, your plumber, or your congressperson . . . anyone could be a birthparent.

One commonly held myth about birthparents is that while on the one hand it is assumed or suggested that they never really wanted their children, there is continued concern that they will some day return to "steal" their children back. The fact of the matter is that while thousands of children are missing each year, there has only been one case, to my knowledge, of a kidnapping of an adopted child in which a birthparent was even suspected, and the charges were dropped because the birthparents had been fighting to overturn the surrender since the child was two months old. Yet the media plays on the unfounded fears of adoptive parents with scare headlines such as "Adoption: Whose Child Is It Anyway?" (See page 32.)

The most publicized case often cited as an example of why adoptive parents must keep their guard up against the possibility of a birthparent lurking behind every bush, ready to "snatch" their child, is the Olga Scarpeta/DeMartino case of the early '70s. This case was erroneously reported by the media and further distorted in the minds of the public. It was the adoptive parents, not the birthmother, who disobeyed a court order and kidnapped the child. Scarpeta surrendered her child to adoption under a great deal of pressure. She then exercised her legal right to reverse that surrender within the legal time limit before the adoption was finalized. A New York State judge granted her request ordering the child, known as Baby Lenore, returned to the natural mother. The prospective adoptive parents, the DeMartinos, fled to Florida ignoring the court order. Lenore remains to this day with the family who kidnapped her, while Scarpeta was judged the villain by the press and public.

Far from intentions of snatching their children away from loving homes, few, if any, birthparents harbor any hope of regaining custody. All searching birthparents want is

33

to know that their children are alive and well and that their children have the kind of lives they were promised: a two-parent, stable household. Those finding children in such a home do nothing to disturb their children's lives. But how can birthparents gain such assurance without agency assistance? Many have found their children in far less than the "perfect" home which was promised them.

"Much of my pain could have been eased if I had known she was alive, healthy and happy, if her adoptive parents had sent updates to the file at the Children's Bureau. Then I could have waited more patiently for her to contact me when she was ready. Because I still don't know anything about her except, finally, that she is alive, I need to see for myself that everything has worked out for her happiness." Sandy Cox, Wilmington, Delaware.

We must lift the veil of secrecy that shrouds adoption in order to shed light on it.

Robert Jay Lifton, psychologist, wrote in his foreword to Mary Benet's *Politics of Adoption:* "The adoption experience cannot be free of dislocated human arrangements. For the most part our society handles the dislocation by offering a substitute family, but at a price. That price is the suppression of the adoptee's 'life story'—the psychological and practical excision of his or her personal history and biological connectedness. What has been excised is replaced by fantasy—the adoptee's, the adoptive parent's, and society's. The fantasy—and I use the term here to suggest solipsistic distortion as opposed to more healthy forms of imagination—begins with the falsification of the birth certificate and extends indefinitely around most of the adoptee's life process.

"There is, thus, a dark side to the adoptive situation. It is a 'dirty little secret' about origins. The essence of that secret is the specter of illegitimacy—the specific illegitimacy of being born out of wedlock, as most adoptees are, together with a kind of secondary illegitimacy in the maneuvers and surreptitious arrangements that bind everyone concerned to secrecy . . ."

34

The idea that there is a dark side to adoption is neither new nor original. This darkness exists wherever adoption records are sealed, ostensibly to protect adoptees from the stigma of illegitimacy. But as Lifton points out, today, secret keeping in and of itself can create more of a stigma than the truth.

"I can remember times when first hearing the word (adoption) would make me cry. I couldn't share my feelings with anybody—I couldn't share the hurt that I felt either. I was locked in a cage of thoughts with no exit. Even if there had been an exit, I don't think it would have mattered. No, it wouldn't have mattered—because it was so dark and I wouldn't have seen it anyway." Paola Breda, adoptee, Ontario, Canada.

And from a birthmother: "I have claustrophobia. I am afraid of closed-in places. I find myself stuck in a closet. I want to come out, but fear bars the door . . . There's only one key to the closet. Knowledge will open the door. If I can find the answer—the truth Will Set Me Free. The Fear will diminish the Light."[15]

The dark veil of secrecy that was intended to protect has enslaved and imprisoned many. The time has come to destroy the myths that lurk in the darkness and replace them with the light of truth and fact.

Part Two

The Facts

"Let us remind ourselves that after all the experience of one's own identity, or becoming a person, is the simplest experience in life even though at the same time the most profound. As everyone knows, a little child will react indignantly and strongly if you, in teasing, call him by the wrong name. It is as though you take away his identity—a most precious thing to him. In the Old Testament the phrase 'I will blot out their names'—to erase their identity and it will be as though they never had existed—is a more powerful threat than physical death."—Rollo May, *Man's Search for Himself*[1]

2

Adoptees:
A Population at Risk

*"We are all of us calling across the incalculable gulfs
which separate us . . ."*—David Grayson

"The figures showing that adopted children do better
than those who stay with their unmarried mothers can be
used by both sides in the argument. The adopters say it vin-
dicates their role; the unmarried mothers, that it proves they
are unfairly treated by society." Mary Benet, *The Politics of
Adoption.*

Though those who promote adoption would have us
believe otherwise, studies indicate that the majority of teen
mothers do not abuse or neglect their children. All statistics
need to be looked at carefully and critically to see how they
are obtained. In the case of child abuse statistics it must be
noted that the scales are tipped against the economically
deprived. Such people often lack the resources to choose
private medical practitioners, and need to rely instead on
public health programs where incidents of this nature are
more likely to be reported. One can only wonder how much
abuse goes unreported daily in the offices of physicians who
are treating the families of their golf partners.

We can recognize the potential of abuse and neglect in a
young, single, possibly unemployed mother; yet many would

39

react with disbelief at the possibility that not only does child abuse span all ethnic groups, races, religions, educational levels and financial strata, but that child abuse actually occurs in adoptive as well as non-adoptive homes. Once we realize some basic facts, however, it becomes more plausible to conceive, understand, and be compassionate of such a phenomenon.

Behavioral biologists, such as Glenn Hausfater of Cornell Medical Center; psychologist Joseph Erwin, director of Mattole Institute in California; Martin Reite, a psychiatrist at the University of Colorado School of Medicine; and Nancy Caine, a Bucknell University psychologist, are just a few of the professionals interested in exploring one particular form of child abuse: stepparent abuse. According to Wilson and Daly, psychologists at McMaster University: "Among the 87,789 validated cases of abused or neglected children reported to the American Humane Association in 1976, stepchildren were two to seven times as likely to be abused, depending upon their ages, as the children living with their biological parents."[2]

Hausfater, noting that infanticide, the most severe form of abuse, is practiced in the animal kingdom by nonrelated males, has coined the phrase "absence of kinship" to explain the similarity between animal abuse and abuse of human children living with non-blood-related parents.

It is important to bear in mind that only a small percentage (five to ten percent) of the acts of child abuse or neglect are perpetuated by pathological parents; "the remainder of child abusers appear to be normal human beings."[3]

Parenting is certainly one of the most challenging professions and one that is entered into with the least amount of preparation. Adoptive parents, as a group, should not be expected to be any better or any worse than any other group of parents equally matched for age, financial resources, etc. Adoption then takes equally matched groups and tips the scales by adding to one set of families the burden of "absence of kinship."

It is true that some people may become parents unexpectedly or by accident, while adoption is a deliberate, often painstaking and sometimes expensive proposition. It is therefore concluded that adoptive parents are generally highly motivated and have a strong desire to parent which may or may not be true of all other parents. This is generally true. However, what is difficult to realize is that motivation and desire alone do not prevent abuse.

If research were carried out carefully and correctly in this area we would be surprised to find that not only is child abuse just as prevalent among adopted as non-adopted parents, I would not be at all surprised to find that it is higher among adoptive parents. Firstly, because of absence of kinship and secondly because of expectations. Those who want to adopt a handicapped child know that they can do so and that they can do so with little or no cost and little or no wait. Many handicapped children are available for adoption with financial aid.

Those who choose to wait years to adopt and/or choose to spend thousands of dollars to adopt privately do so because they want a healthy, white newborn. They want a "perfect" child; they do not want a handicapped child, an older child or a non-white child. But adoption holds no guarantees for anyone and there are a disproportionately high number of adopted children with learning disabilities, hyperactivity and other acting-out disorders, many of which are not evident until school age.

What happens to the couple, already under stress because of their infertility, years of doctors probing, perhaps surgery, feeling degraded by adoption agencies, feeling dehumanized, feeling as if they have to "prove themselves" . . . what happens when you add to such an already stressed family a non-related child? What happens to their expectations when, after a large investment of time, emotion and money their dream child has a behavioral problem?

The 1987 beating death of six-year-old Elizabeth "Lisa" Steinberg, the child placed for adoption with New York attorney Joel Steinberg and his common-law wife, Hedda Nussbaum, was an extreme example of what can happen. When police responded to the emergency call they found Lisa naked and bruised with her forehead and temple crush-

Battered girl ruled brain dead;

adoptive father faces murder charges

NEW YORK (AP)—A 6-year-old girl, allegedly battered into a coma by her adoptive father in their blood-spattered, filthy Manhattan home, was pronounced dead last night.

The death of Elizabeth Steinberg, who had been unconscious since she was found by police Monday, means Joel Barnet Steinberg will be charged with murder, said Assistant District Attorney John Fried.

The girl was declared legally dead at St. Vincent's Hospital when a second brain scan showed no activity, said William Grinker, head of the city Human Resources Administration. He made the announcement at a Manhattan news conference where he defended his agency's role in the case.

Police discovered the battered child and her 16-month-old brother after their mother, Hedda Nussbaum, phoned police Monday to report an emergency.

Nussbaum, who has lived with Steinberg 17 years and was herself the alleged victim of his beatings, told police Elizabeth had choked on food and was having trouble breathing.

Hospital officials said the girl had suffered bleeding in the brain and bruises to the head and spine. She was kept alive on a respirator until yesterday. Fried said earlier yesterday the child was officially pronounced "brain dead" but would not be disconnected from the respirator until a court-appointed legal guardian authorized the move.

At 8:45 p.m., the hospital issued a statement without elaborating: "Elizabeth Steinberg has expired. The case is under the jurisdiction of the New York City medical examiner."

Residents of the building, some insisting on anonymity, maintained authorities were called fre... beatings of Nussbaum.

Screams and ...

aparim...

"every o...

"getting... Neighbors Say Abuse Was Reported

Vicki Pol...

the same f...

"Who protected this child?" asked Polon. "No one. And they got to adopt another child. It's horrible—unbelievable."

The Manhattan district attorney is investigating whether the two children were legally adopted by Steinberg, 46, who is being held without bail. The criminal lawyer pleaded innocent Tuesday night to charges of attempted murder, assault and endangering the welfare of his two adopted children, Elizabeth and Mitchell.

Police found the adopted boy tethered to a chair and wallowing in his own excrement. But doctors at St. Vincent's Hospital said he was in good shape and the boy was turned over to HRA for foster placement.

Nussbaum, 45, a children's book author, former editor and former teacher, was in the prison ward at Elmhurst Hospital in Queens, facing the same charges as Steinberg.

A grand jury will hear evidence

today regarding the murder charge against Steinberg; no decision has been made on additional charges against Nussbaum, Fried said.

Greenwich Village neighbors of the couple said the injuries she was being treated for were inflicted by Steinberg in repeated beatings over a long period.

THE NEW YORK TIMES, WEDNESDAY, NOVEMBER 4, 1987

... for the ... that Nussbaum's condition was stable and that doctors have ruled out surgery for her ulcerated leg in favor of treatment with antibiotics.

'There were authorities, people in power, who did nothing.'

Police and the city welfare department initially said they had only one prior complaint against the couple. But Grinker told a crowded news conference his agency received complaints of child neglect in 1983 and child abuse in 1984 involving Steinberg and his daughter.

In both instances, investigations by his office—including a check of the girl for signs of abuse—produced findings of no problems, Grinker said. Records of the first case have been de-

stroyed, but papers on the second were discovered, he said.

"The caseworker did the job very carefully (in 1984), but in hindsight, obviously they hid something," said Grinker. "... The records show the house was a decent house, and the child was taken care of."

Police responded to an anonymous call Oct. 6 and found that Nussbaum had been hit in the face but refused to press charges, said Deputy Inspector Robert Frankel.

Two assistant district attorneys were checking through records of Surrogate and Family courts for paperwork that would show whether Steinberg had l... ...ted the ch...

... narcotics in ...e apartment, said Gloria montealegre, speaking for the district attorney's office.

Investigators said they found $25,000, quantities of cocaine, hashish and marijuana and drug paraphernalia in the apartment, which they described as a filthy, bloodstained shambles.

"I understand there were drugs. Something, perhaps, is the matter with society," said Grinker when asked how something like this could happen. "I don't think a government agency is responsible every time something goes wrong in a person's private life."

The two-bedroom apartment is on the third floor of a townhouse on West 10th Street off Fifth Avenue that was once the residence of Mark Twain.

6-year-old had been in a coma; N.Y. agencies defend actions

Private adoption safeguards are questioned.

ed. She was brought to the hospital in a coma, where she was pronounced brain dead and later dead. Also in the filthy, blood-stained apartment was the couple's other illegally adopted child, Mitchell, age sixteen months, tethered by a rope around his waist to a piece of furniture in the living room, soiled with urine and excrement and drinking from a bottle of spoiled milk. Also found in the apartment were marijuana and cocaine.

In the days that followed there were charges of murder brought against Steinberg and Nussbaum and there were many questions: How and why did people like this adopt? Were the adoptions legal? What precautions do we have to prevent the illegal transfer of children?

Lisa's mother, Michelle Launders, was nineteen and unmarried at the time of her pregnancy and wanted her child to have advantages she could not afford. Her doctor referred her to an attorney named Steinberg to make the arrangements. Michelle's mother paid Steinberg their last five hundred dollars to place the child in a good home. They had no idea that he was to be the "adoptive father." "If I had wanted my daughter killed," Michelle said, "I would have had an abortion."

Mitchell's mother, Nicole Smigiel, age seventeen, had gone into labor the same day her pregnancy was confirmed. No one knew except Nicole and her mother. The same doctor who confirmed the pregnancy delivered Mitchell and told Nicole and her mother that he had a friend, an attorney, who could "take care of everything." Within seven hours of knowing that Nicole was pregnant, Nicole and her mother signed adoption papers produced by Attorney David Verplank.

Verplank admitted representing Nicole. He knew the Steinbergs (a couple who had been reported to the police and social services for family violence since 1983) and in 1985 gave them the child. Verplank claims he told the Steinbergs that they would have to marry in order to finalize the adoption and claims they said that they would. That was the end of Verplank's representation of his client, Nicole Smigiel. He never checked to see if the Steinbergs married, which they did not; nor did he or anyone else ever check Mitchell's living conditions; nor did he or anyone else ever check to see if the adoption was finalized, which it was not. After sixteen months in what became known as "the Greenwich Village house of horror" Mitchell's custody was returned to his mother, Nicole. Michelle Launders was granted permission to bury her daughter. As you will see in Chapter Five, this was done only because neither adoption was finalized.

Was this an isolated case, a fluke that fell through the cracks of an otherwise good system, or does the system have major flaws which need revamping? The placement of Mitchell into a drug-ridden, violent family could never have happened if the State of New York (and other states) had provided more stringent restrictions on adoptions, such as not allowing one attorney to represent both the birth and adoptive parents, and a follow-up system to see to it that procedures were followed. While lax regulations on private adoptions are clearly to blame for Mitchell's placement, it is presumable that the Steinbergs may have appeared stable enough six years prior to have qualified through legal channels to adopt their first child. Many adoptions which start out fine end in tragedy. While home studies can prevent obvious problems, there are no guarantees. Adoption abuse takes place in both private and agency adoptions.

William "Billy" Roher III came to this country from South America only three months before his death on May 28, 1975 at the age of two and one-half. His death, caused by a concussion to the head, was originally reported as an accident by Mimi Roher, the wife of a New Jersey township mayor who was charged with the murder of her adopted son. Roher claimed that the boy was "not normal" and that his death resulted from his falling from a chair. The forty-three year old wife of the seventy-three year old mayor was brought to trial when the allegedly self-inflicted bite marks were discovered even on the boy's jaw. Roher, who now lives with her twelve year old adopted daughter since her separation from her husband, jumped bail once, and was returned for a trial which ended in a hung jury.

Another isolated case? Perhaps. But in May, 1982, Old Bridge, New Jersey Councilwoman Sonja Fineberg and her husband, Arnold, were charged by the Middlesex County Prosecutor's Office with endangering the welfare of their fourteen year old son by inflicting unusually severe corporal punishment. The Fineberg's younger son was treated at Old Bridge Regional Hospital for welts and bruises on his back, while the couple claimed they had tried their best to give loving guidance to their two adopted sons.

These cases came readily to light while I was collecting data for this book; however, there is no reason to assume that adoption abuse is more common on the East Coast than elsewhere. Dr. Martin Palmer of Primary Children's Hospital in Salt Lake City, Utah, for instance, reports seeing more child abuse among his patients who are adopted than in those who are not. The following newsclippings illustrate that adoption abuse holds no geographical boundaries:

". . . A lawyer and his wife were charged today with locking their adopted teenage son in a tiny cage in their basement."—United Press International, St. Louis, 1984.

"An adopted teenager being punished by his parents was forced to live in a three by four-foot crate, say police who found the barefoot youth hunched and shivering in a basement so cold police officers could see their breath . . . The parents, Howard, 37, and Marjorie Munson, 33, were charged with child abuse in what one police officer called 'the worst case of child abuse we have ever investigated' . . . The youth, Alonso Richard Munson, is between thirteen and fifteen years old, a native of Colombia, South America, and was adopted by the Munsons a year and a half ago."—Associated Press, Clayton, MO, 22 November, 1983.

"A truck driver got permission from his estranged wife to take their two preschoolers to a discount store, but instead drove just northwest of town, walked one hundred feet into the woods and hanged himself and the children, authorities said . . . They were identified as

Dead boy called 'not normal'

CAMDEN (AP) — The wife of the Haddon Township mayor, on trial in the murder of her 2½-year-old adopted son, described the youngster as abnormal and "self-destructive" and said that the behavior led to his death, the defense attorney says.

But the prosecutor countered by arguing that repeated physical abuse caused the death of the child, whose body was marked by bites.

The Superior Court jury of nine women and six men heard opening arguments yest the trial of Mimi Rohrer, 43. Testimon continue today, and the trial is expected t

1975 death of the child, William Jr. Because of the long period between the death and the indictment, the only charge open to the grand jury was murder, rather than the manslaughter charges often filed in child abuse cases, prosecutors said.

Deputy Attorney General Anthony Zarrillo said in his opening statement that the findings of the first autopsy on the boy were incomplete — that former Camden County Medical Examiner Dr. William Read noticed bruises on the boy's

Hung jury ends N.J. murder trial

A mistrial was declared Monday in the murder case of **Mimi Rohrer**, the wife of Haddon Township, N.J.'s Mayor **William Rohrer**.

She was accused of killing the couple's 3½-year-old adopted son, **William Rohrer III**, in 1975.

The 12 jurors were dismissed by Superior Court Judge **David Eynon** after they failed to reach a verdict in the 13-week trial.

ROHRER: Mayor's wife accused of killing adopted son

Mom extradited in boy's slaying

CAMDEN (AP) — Mimi Rohrer, arrested in Philadelphia last week after failing to appear at her trial here on charges of murdering her adopted son, was returned to New Jersey in handcuffs yesterday.

The wife of Haddon Township Mayor William G. Rohrer Jr. is accused of subjecting their adopted son to physical abuse that eventually killed him in 1975 at two years old.

Mimi Rohrer, 43, had been free on

her defense attorney, Raymond M. Brown.

"There is nothing wrong with me," Rohrer told reporters after her extradition hearing.

She added that she believed her civil rights were being violated because Eynon on Oct. 5 denied her request to replace Brown with Tinari as her defense attorney.

"I tried to fire him, but I can't," she told reporters outside Hirsh's court-

Rohrer free on bail posted by husband

CAMDEN (AP) — Mimi Rohrer, who fled the state last month during her trial on charges of killing her adopted son, was released on bail yesterday, and the judge warned her would continue her trial without her if she fails to show up.

Superior Court Judge David G. Eynon set bail at $100,000 and said Mrs. Rohrer could be released from Camden County Jail if she posted 10 percent of her bail, or $10,000. She was released after her husband presented a cashier's check.

Mrs. Rohrer is charged with subjecting 2½-year-old William Rohrer III to physical abuse that eventually resulted in his death three months after he arrived from El Salvador.

Eynon granted defense attorney

would make sure his wife appears at her trial.

Rohrer, 74, who has been separated from his 43-year-old wife, would leave the Haddon Township apartment where he has been staying and would return to the couple's Westmont home, said Brown.

He added that the couple's 12-year-old adopted daughter, Laura, who has been staying with a friend of Mrs. Rohrer's in western Pennsylvania, would also return to the family's home.

Mrs. Rohrer's brother, Mark Mungello, also pledged to make sure the defendant appears at her trial.

Deputy Attorney General Anthony Zarrillo opposed the request for bail, citing her flight across state lines

MIMI ROHRER
... charged in son's death

Adopted girl lauds mom at child-abuse trial

CAMDEN (AP) — The 11-year-old adopted daughter of a woman charged with causing the 1975 death of her adopted son testified as the final defense witness yesterday, telling the jury her relationship with her mother was "great."

Laura Rohrer also said she did not remember her stepbrother, Billy, whom authorities allege died as a result of continued physical abuse

son's death. Defense attorney Raymond M. Brown said early in the case that the child was "self-destructive."

Miss Rohrer, called as the last witness before Brown rested his case in Superior Court here, testified for 11 minutes, but could not answer questions about Billy.

"I don't know him," she replied when Brown asked if she had any re-

er hits me. She's a good mother."

Superior Court Judge David G. Eynon scheduled summations by attorneys in the case for tomorrow.

The medical examiner initially attributed the boy's death to "severe contusions of the brain" as the result of a fall from a high chair.

But a 1977 report by the State Commission of Investigation said there were discrepancies in Mrs.

they hold her under
Zarrillo said. "I don't
tive they would be if
er mind to take off

Keith Hays Greer, forty-two, Christie Lynn Greer, five, and Keith Wayne Greer, three, all of Pine Bluff . . . the young boy was the couple's natural son, and . . . Greer adopted the girl when she was three months old."—Associated Press, Pine Bluff, AR, November, 1984.

". . . Mary Beth Tinning, forty-three, was charged with suffocating her daughter Tami Lynne, three and a half months . . . police said they had opened an investigation into the suspicious deaths of eight other infants in the family in fourteen years . . . the youngest was eight days old . . . the oldest four years . . . eight of the dead children were Tinning's natural children, and one was a baby she wanted to adopt . . . through a private agency but at the time of his death had not finalized the process."—Inquirer News Service, Schenectady, NY, 1986.

"Woman, sixty-one, charged with murder of three year old son adopted in 1965. Lois Jurgens of Stillwater, Minnesota, pleaded innocent to charges that she beat her adopted son to death. 'He died a very tragic death, a very brutal death and that's why his adoptive mother is standing trial,' said Tom Foley, Ramsey County Attorney."—*Courier News,* 31 January, 1987. (Jurgens was subsequently found guilty thanks, in part, to the testimony of her former foster children. Jurgens had adopted through a municipal agency.) (See also, Chapter Five.)

". . . Linda Burnes surrendered her son Allen in the belief that adoption would provide him with a better life than she could offer. Later, a Florida caseworker called to tell her that he was in the hospital in critical condition after falling in a hot bathtub in his new family's home. Five days later her son died, and the adopting mother was charged with manslaughter."—*Communicator,* CUB.

Some may suggest that reporting such case histories is sensationalizing because the vast majority of adopted people lead healthy, happy, and well cared-for lives. In fact, the vast majority of *all* children lead relatively happy and safe lives. It is the minority who do not that child abuse regulations seek to protect. This minority includes adopted and non-adopted children. Further, for every reported case of violence and abuse, we must recognize how many more go unreported. Though each of us may ourselves be fortunate to have been spared an abusive childhood, and may not know of any such acts within our own circle of friends and family, we cannot deny the fact that four out of ten children will be sexually molested before reaching majority.

Physical abuse, while the most likely to receive coverage in the news media, is not the only form of abuse to which children are subjected. Sexual abuse, though less often reported, is not excluded from adoptive homes. Due to a lack of thorough research in this area, it is not known whether the absence of an incest taboo results in a marked increase in sexual abuse in adoptive, foster and stepparent homes as compared to children living with both biological parents, as suggested by the following newspaper excerpts:

". . . the father is said to have apologized to his adopted daughter after the rape . . . The incident allegedly occurred between October 6 and 7, 1983. A 13-year-old girl told a detective that her adoptive father came into her bedroom at home and raped her . . ."—*St. Petersburg Times,* FL, 1984.

". . . George and Betty Warnock of Des Moines, Iowa were found guilty of twelve counts each of neglect and abandonment of children by locking infants and toddlers in tiny wooden boxes, handcuffing and stripping a mentally retarded foster child and sexually abusing a foster child. The Warnocks are adoptive parents of four other children."—*Des Moines Register.*

". . . Ronald Duane Ferrin, thirty-five, shot himself with the same pistol used to kill his adopted daughter and critically wound his wife. Court files show Mrs. Ferrin claimed her husband had beaten and raped her and abused their children . . ."—Associated Press, Clarkston.

". . . A seventeen year old girl shot her adoptive father, Thomas Buttweiler, to death as he slept three years ago after a long history of sexual and physical abuse."—Newsclipping of unknown origin, courtesy of Concerned United Birthparents.

". . . for Jane, seventeen, survival means a shabby basement apartment and the birth next month of a baby she says is her adoptive father's. Jane has been on her own since April, just one month after her seventeenth birthday. Her adoptive parents separated and both have moved out of the state . . . Jane says she has a lot to forget: a natural mother who gave her away, a childhood spent in foster homes, an adoptive father who began sexually abusing her when she was eight, and an adoptive mother who was too distraught over the pending divorce to take care of her daughter when Jane finally told her about the years of abuse."—"The 'Throwaway' Children," *Newsday,* 18 November, 1984.

"A Rockland County man, named an Illinois Adoptive Parent of the Year for adopting five former foster children, pleaded guilty Thursday in Circuit Court to sexually assaulting one of his children. David Wells, fifty-six . . . was sentenced . . . to ten years in prison for the criminal sexual assault of his sixteen year old adopted son . . . The five children, who range in age from eleven to sixteen, were taken in to DYFS custody . . . One of the children was a victim of Down's syndrome, and some of the others also had handicaps . . . Wells repeatedly abused the sixteen year old boy and had isolated incidents of sexual contact with other children . . . Wells was granted custody of the children in a divorce settlement."—*The Rockford Register Star,* 7 November, 1986.

"An adoptive father in Huntsville, Alabama, was convicted of the first degree rape of his nine year old mentally retarded daughter. James Goode was charged with child sexual abuse and rape for repeatedly raping the girl over several months."—*The Birmingham News,* 24 April, 1987.

There is, too, emotional abuse to which many children—adopted children included—are subjected. Many an adopted person has found out the truth of his adopted status in the midst of an angry parent/child confrontation. The present system of sealed records begins with the issuance of a fraudulent amended birth certificate which states that the child was born to his adoptive parents. The sealed record system is based on lies and therefore encourages dishonesty.

"Though countless books encourage parents to be honest with their children lest they undermine their trust, the child welfare experts encourage just the opposite," said Margaret McDonald Lawrence in a 1979 presentation to the American Adoption Congress. "In their view, dishonesty is the best policy in adoption and this aberration can be rationalized on the grounds that the end justifies the means. The end, of course, is a legitimate family. Perhaps the social work position is a reflection of the societal view that the biological family is the only legitimate family. But child welfare workers reveal their own lack of faith in non-biological relationships by their manipulation of people in an adoption to create the illusion of a biological relationship. Obviously they do not really believe that unrelated parents and children can be a legitimate family without simulated, since not natural, blood ties. The child's origin and past must be obscured so that there will be no existing and competing blood ties. A new birth certificate must be created that falsely leaves claim to another child's name and falsely declares the new parents to be progenitors." This falsified certificate can then set a foundation of lies which seem to justify the adoptive parents' right to withhold the truth from their adopted children.

Perhaps the cruelest form of emotional abuse perpetrated on adopted youths is using the adoption as a threat: "If you're bad, we'll send you back." Whether said outright, in anger, or more subtly, the message is given and/or received. Indeed, shocking as it might seem, some adopted children *are* "given back." The following letter, dated July 23, 1984, was sent to ORIGINS, NJ:

"Dear Sir:
"About five and one half years ago we adopted a little girl through DSS. I won't go into all the details, but it is not working out too well. I feel it would be better for her with her natural mother. What I want to know is if you can locate her (the natural mother) for me. All they told us is that she was given up at age three months.
"Enclosed is an addressed, stamped envelope.
"Sincerely, Mrs. C.P.B., Darlington, SC."

This is not an isolated case, as the following examples illustrate:

"There should be a chapter in Jill Krementz's book[4] called 'The Darker Side of Being Adopted.' I was adopted at six months by an upper-middle-class couple. I was never told I was adopted, and at thirteen, when I found out, my 'parents' denied it. I tried to approach the subject but was constantly threatened with disinheritance or that, if I misbehaved, I would be shipped back to the adoption agency. Do I thank the Lord every day for being chosen by these people? I think not. I was adopted to fulfill the social requirements of these people. A new Cadillac would have served the same purpose. Name Withheld, Tucson."—*People,* 6 December, 1982.

". . . A Miami adoptive couple spent two years trying to get rid of the adopted son they considered a 'trouble-maker' . . . The adoptive father, Tom Deft, was quoted as saying, 'We've been actively trying to get rid of him for two years,' before Judge Adele Segall Faske issued an order to cancel the adoption."—Newspaper clipping of unknown origin, courtesy of Concerned United Birthparents.

Elizabeth Cole, adoption specialist with Children's Welfare League of America states: "We are witnessing an increase in disruptions and there seems to be an increase in disruptions happening in adolescence (in cases) where the child was adopted as an infant. That's really the shocker. It corresponds to a new sense today that parents can divorce their kids."[5]

A glance through the books of "hard to place" children available at many adoption agencies today reveals tale after tale of "disrupted" adoptions—a polite euphemism for failure. Yet, while the state of New Jersey, for instance, keeps track of how many Division of Youth and Family Services (DYFS) adoptive placements are disrupted before being finalized, the number that break down after adoptions are finalized is unknown. The state also does not keep figures on the number of disruptions that occur after placement by private as opposed to state agencies or non-agency adoptions.

"Joell was adopted as an infant, but the adoptive parents placed her in a home for handicapped children when she was four. There is suspicion of early abuse. Joell is nine and in foster care awaiting a permanent home, again."—*The Cap Book, Inc.,* 700 Exchange Street, Rochester, NY 14608.

"Jason, fourteen, is a healthy, active, creative Jewish boy of above-average intelligence. He is college material, artistic, and plays guitar. After the death of Jason's adoptive father, his adoptive mother terminated her parental rights."—Lutheran Family Services, 33 Worth Street, New York, NY 10013.

"Tommy, eleven years old, is currently living in a group home. Tommy is an interracial boy who has experienced many placements, including a disrupted adoption . . ."—New York State *Blue Book.*

"Danny and Darlene are siblings born in 1968 and 1969 . . . These children have recently undergone an adoption disruption . . ."—New York State *Blue Book.*

"Patrick is a twelve year old boy with a slight build. He is highly intelligent and earns high grades in school . . . Patrick recently experienced an adoption disruption . . ."—Open Door Society of Long Island, P.O. Box 236, Ronkonkama, NY 11779.

"Lisa was born in 1975 and is currently on medication to control her hyperactivity . . . Lisa has been through one unsuccessful adoption . . ."—Open Door Society of Long Island.

Helen Pritchard (birthmother) was reunited with one of her twin sons, Keith McGuire, on "Hour Magazine"[6] in 1984. Tragically, her other son had passed away several years previously—after trying to locate her for vital medical information. Keith was overjoyed to have been found. His adoptive mother had died when the twins were nine. They and their adopted sister were passed around from adoptive relative to relative until their adoptive father remarried. At thirteen, their stepmother culminated years of bad relationships by tossing them back into the system. From then on it was courts, welfare, group homes, and finally foster care. Scott and Keith were interviewed by "Hour Magazine" when the program did a segment honoring their foster mother, who had cared for more than 1,500 children. Scott died one month later.[7]

As you can see, some of these adoption breakdowns occurred as the result of the death or divorce of the adoptive parents. Recent studies indicate that family stress such as death, divorce, alcohol and drug abuse is resulting in large numbers of teenage "throw aways" among both adopted and non-adopted youth.[8] While family breakup as a result of such tragedies is perhaps understandable, and requires its own solutions, some of the causes of break-up in adoptive families are unique as compared to non-adopted families and some possible preventative measures are explored in Chapter Six.

Abuse occurs in a minority of adoptive and non-adoptive families, but there are unique difficulties facing all adopted persons. Adoptees, even those raised in stable and loving homes, experience problems unlike their non-adopted counterparts. Many report feeling incomplete, not whole, as if a piece of the puzzle were missing. Melissa Norvell and Rebecca F. Guy observe: "He may view himself as only half a person, the other half being obscured by his adoption. This perception of a less than adequate background may provoke feelings of inferiority, guilt, and insecurity. These feelings, coupled with identity diffusion, can contribute to a more negative self-concept in the adopted adolescent."[9]

> "I always had a big empty space inside me that made me feel unreal," Walter, "Why So Many Adoptions Fail," Bernard Asbell, *Good Housekeeping,* August, 1962.

Adoptees also express feeling out of control of their lives. They may feel as if secret pacts were made over them, about them, and for them, over which they had no control then and still do not in most states today. Still others resent the fact that they are forever kept, legally and often socially, adopted "children." Many strongly object to being treated like second class citizens who are denied the same right granted all other citizens, the right to their birth records. Jean Paton, an adoptee, former social worker and author, said in an interview, "I think that adopted people have a tremendous feeling of inferiority, a feeling of not belonging . . . I think of us," she said, "as 'social orphans' who lost parents, not by death, but by social decision."[10]

Others express feeling as if they were hatched, not born; feeling alien, unconnected to the human race. Many adoptees I have met express extreme joy in becoming the parents of their own children and thus having, for the first time in their lives, someone who is related to them and looks like them. For others the prospect of childbearing can be fear provoking. Betty Jean Lifton, adoptee and author,[11] found that female adoptees express increased concern over genetic factors when they marry or reach childbearing age.

Pam Hasegawa, New Jersey State Coordinator of ALMA, describes her experience: "When they put my infant daughter in my arms I was overwhelmed with grief that I had never had a chance to know my mother and that she had to give me up."[12]

S. Farber concluded a longitudinal study of twenty-one children, nineteen of whom were adopted. He found "two consistent patterns—girls manifest greater interest and conflict in relation to adoption than do boys, and interest and conflict are greatest for both sexes during latency."[13] Reinforcement of the idea that females are "more interested" than males has appeared to come from the fact that adoption search groups nationwide have a predominance of female members as compared to male. However, one cannot make such assumptions because children do change when they become adults and many men simply attack the situation differently than by joining groups and attending meetings. Some male adoptees do express hostility that may become generalized to all women, but in my work with searching male adoptees and birthparents, I have come to some interesting conclusions.

In the late 1970s, when I first became involved with adoption search groups, I was impressed with the predominance of female adoptees in search. When we first began ORIGINS, an organization for women who have lost children to adoption, we prepared those birthmothers who chose to initiate search by telling them that male adoptees appear to be less interested in their origins than do females. This has proven to be an incorrect interpretation of the facts.

Fewer male adoptees may actively initiate search for their birthfamilies but there has been no distinct difference in the reactions of adult adoptees found by their birthfamilies based on gender. Male adoptees are just as glad as females to be found. Though my experience with male adoptees has been limited, those with whom I have worked have been, if anything, more zealous and more impassioned in their quest for their birthfamilies than are some female adoptees. Whether adoptees are glad to be found or not depends more upon other factors in their upbringing than on their gender.

One deciding factor is how and when they were told of their adoption. Often the later one discovers the truth, the more hostility toward the adoptive parents for withholding vital information. A late in life revelation can often destroy trust and loyalty, therefore lessening any taboo, real or imagined, on search.

Other factors which determine whether adoptees are likely to pursue a search or not include the direct or subliminal messages the adoptee receives throughout life in regard to the subject of adoption. Those who have been told that they were surrendered out of love appear to have higher self-esteem and carry less hostility and resentment. Adoptees' natural desire to quench their curiosity through search was once thought of as a slap in the face of the parents who raised them. This is not so. It is often the adoptee who feels more secure in his parent's love who has the courage to undertake such an expedition into the past.

One wonders why, with approximately 6,000 different genetically transmitted diseases (according to the Heredity Disease Foundation) affecting an estimated fifteen million Americans, one would need to be secure in order to search. Anyone who has ever been asked by a doctor if there is a history of heart disease, high blood pressure, diabetes or cancer in his family knows why the need for accurate and updated medical information is a major concern of adopted persons. Another less recognized concern of adopted persons and a contributing factor to the very real need for search is fear of unknowingly committing incest. Farfetched though this may sound, it is indeed a very real possibility. There have been reported cases of mothers marrying sons, and sisters and brothers discovering their biological relationship only after becoming engaged or married. Fear of incest was reportedly a major reason that Israel opened its sealed adoption records in 1960.

"A man who married his mother was indicted on incest charges yesterday by a grand jury that concluded he was lying when he said he didn't know they were related . . . Danny James Bass, twenty-six, was surrendered for adoption . . . and had claimed that he discovered a few months after the wedding that Mary Ann Bass, forty-three, was his mother."—Associated Press, Charlotte, TN, 1984.

Is it any wonder that living with a void for medical history and unknowns for kin, adoption would add stress to one's life? As a result of feelings of rejection and difficulty with identity formation, Schecter (1960) noted that adopted children are more apt to develop neurotic and psychotic states than are non-adopted children. Adoptees are over-represented tenfold among people in therapy with respect to their frequency in the overall population. That is, although only two percent of the population is adopted, ten to twenty percent or more of those in therapy are adopted.

While many residential facilities do not ask whether children being admitted are adopted or not, The Haven, a residential treatment center for twelve to eighteen year olds, reports that seventy to eighty percent of its population is adopted.[14] These figures are echoed at other teen units such as the one at Coldwater Canyon's Center for Personal Development, Southern California. Dr. Lee Bloom, the unit's director reports "an alarmingly high percentage are adopted—sixty to eighty-five percent."[15] Likewise, M. Bohman and Al Van Knorring gathered statistics on 2,323 Scandinavian adoptees and found a significantly higher frequency of psychiatric illness among adoptees compared with non-adopted controls. The adoptees had an over-representation in alcohol, drug abuse and personality disorders in both male and female groups than did the non-adopted.[16]

David Brodzinsky, a psychologist who has worked extensively with adoptees, notes that these are not the adoptees we might expect to see in therapy. They are not children who have been through multiple placements, but rather they are adoptees who had been placed as infants.

In contrast to Shecter's findings, John Triseliotis found that while adopted children manifest more personality and behavioral disorders than non-adopted children, in non-adopted children the predominent diagnoses were neurosis and psychosis. It is believed that this is why the dispropor-

57

tionately high number of adopted youths in therapy drops off once they reach adulthood.

The National Committee for Adoption believes that the reason so many adoptees are in therapy is because adoptive parents are more affluent, better educated and tend to seek professional help more readily. Whether this is true or not, adopted children suffer an increased incidence of psychopathology and are, therefore, commonly seen in consultation and therapy.[17] Triseliotis quotes numerous psychiatric studies and observations that adopted children are more likely to have emotional and social problems than non-adopted children and that many scholars report a rather serious degree of disturbance in the adoptive clients coming for psychiatric help.[18]

E.E. Wellisch, psychiatrist, found that the cause of maladjustment in adopted children is "lack of knowledge of their real parents and ancestors . . . The loss of this tradition is a deprivation which may result in the stunting of emotional development." Dr. William Reynolds, in his study published in the '70s, found that adoptees differ most from others in their significantly higher anxiety and their external locus of control, their sense that they are not in charge of their lives.

A teacher, who was herself an adoptee, claimed that she could always tell in a new class of forty five-year-olds which children were adopted because they were over-anxious to please; would take one's hand and seemed insecure; if scolded, would say "I'm sorry, I'm so sorry"; looked suspiciously at the other children; were often anxious about small possessions.[19] Jean Paton's findings concur. Paton finds most adoptees to be passive, hostile and dependent.

As with any stress, adoption can affect different people in different ways and to different degrees. Male adoptees appear to deal with their feelings of rejection with more rage and aggressions than do females. The ultimate expression of such rage is acts of violence, even murder.

". . . Psychologist Ronald Bergman and other specialists have filed reports portraying the young murder suspect as a disturbed child pushed to excel in an adoptive home simultaneously wracked with emotional and marital problems . . . Kenneth was denied use of the telephone, weekend television, and was only allowed to leave his room for school, meals and to use the bathroom. Kenneth reported that both parents often told him that he was only as good as his worst grades . . ."—*The Miami Herald,* FL, 1984.

"A twenty-eight year old Rockland County, New York man who killed his grandfather and critically wounded his grandmother before being gunned down by police Saturday night, was upset with their plans to sell the family home . . . Richard Losicco lived with his adoptive grandparents, Pasquale and Anna Losicco, since the death of his adoptive father, Anthony Losicco in a plane crash in 1982. Another adopted son, twenty year old Terrence Losicco, is serving a twenty-seven and one-half year to life sentence for the 1980 murder of Eleanor Prouty . . . 'Apparently Richard was upset over where he would live once they sold the house,' the district attorney said."—Newspaper clipping of unknown origin, Len Maniace, Staff Writer.

"Donald and Delphine Wright were determined to find their daughter's murderer . . . now their eighteen year old adopted son, Mitchell, a well-liked altar boy who was 'always trying to help' . . . awaits sentencing for the April 12 slaying . . . Mitchell turned viciously on sixteen year old Donette, first setting her up to be raped by a friend and then leaving her to die, beaten and bloodied, under a log . . . Donette and Mitchell were two of four children adopted by the Wrights, who couldn't have children of their own . . . Donette was half Mexican, and the Wrights say Mitchell became hostile toward blacks and Hispanics after learning his natural mother had given birth to a black baby and kept the child after putting him up for adoption."—*The News Journal,* 2 April, 1985.

"The author of *Saul's Book,* Paul T. Rogers, was beaten to death in his Queens, New York apartment by his adopted and disabled son and a friend of the son . . ."—*Publishers Weekly.*

"I had this picture in my mind of me stabbing Marina," (said) Kenneth Baer . . . charged with attempting to murder his former girlfriend . . . "I loved her," he said. "She was my lover, my mother, my everything." The graduate of Thomas Jefferson University, Philadelphia, said he was adopted at a very young age and has been looking for his mother ever since. He said he hit Marina, forty-five, because he loved her. Baer said he frequently hit his ex-wife in the stomach and chest. He was divorced in 1982. He said he hit his adoptive mother several times when he was between the ages of twelve and fifteen. He said he always felt lonely and rejected by women until he met Marina. Baer felt he was losing Marina when she moved out of his apartment."— *The Home News,* NJ, 13 September, 1985.

". . . A fifteen year old Mineral Point youth was sentenced for the slaying of his adoptive parents and brother by multiple stab wounds . . . The youth found out a year ago that he was adopted and he was told his natural parents didn't want him. His natural mother was labled a whore and other degrading statements were made about her and this bothered him and he began to resent his family . . . The defense attorney also said his father, a former boxer, used a discipline regime to extremes, often hitting the youth in the face, stomach and ribs."—*The Capital Times,* 1983.

"Family and friends say Joseph 'Jay' Forman, the sixteen year old charged with murdering Janice Grifone, has long been a 'problem' for his family . . . They also describe the hyperactive youth as a boy who was eager to please but who constantly felt rejected—a feeling perhaps rooted in anxiety over his discovery at the age of eleven that he had been adopted as an infant."—*Trenton Times,* NJ, 26 May, 1982.

"A Queens honor student who hoped to get an appointment to the U.S. Naval Academy was charged yesterday with beating his adoptive mother to death with a baseball bat during an argument over his grades . . . Neighbors describe George Miller, Jr., eighteen, as 'the all-American boy.' Miller won top honors at John Adams High School . . . but his grades did not qualify him for appointment to the Annapolis, Maryland school . . . The young Miller had led a sheltered life . . . to the point that his father had to drive him to a dinner dance . . . a school guidance counselor said Mrs. Miller enrolled him in the more demanding courses, and the counselor said, 'he was a fine young man, respectful, courteous and pleasant. I would be happy to have him as a son.' "—*New York Post,* 12 January, 1985, p. 5.

In *The Shoemaker,* [20] author Flora Rheta Schreiber illustrates in great detail an extreme, though true, case of adoption abuse. Separation anxiety, accompanied by constant and ever-present fear of rejection induced by threats of being returned, coupled with abuse and psychological castration by adoptive parents who were almost old enough to be their son's grandparents and had no understanding of children (they wanted the child to inherit the family business and to take care of them in their old age), led Joseph Kallinger of Pennsylvania to become a psychotic rapist and murderer.

"Joe," says Schreiber, "had come to the Kallinger home as a healthy baby of twenty-two months. The seeds of his adult schizophrenia were sown there. When he left at fifteen, the seeds were already sprouting and he was on his way to the severe paranoid schizophrenia he has had as an adult. He had been the more vulnerable to the abuses of his adoptive parents because of the insecurity and rage, born of abandonment, which he brought to their house. But it was not the first twenty-two months of Joe's life nor a genetic defect that created his psychosis . . . Clearly, in Joe's case, 'the bad seed' is to be found not in nature but in nurture. And yet, though every human contact seemed destined to lead him to the final paroxysm of terror, it was, in retrospect," as Professor Schreiber tells us," not only predictable, but preventable." Schreiber further told me that while Kallinger's natural mother would not have been a model parent, and one cannot speculate how his life would have been or could have been, had he been able to remain with her he would not have suffered the feelings of rejection that wreaked havoc in his life.

The Encyclopedia of Crime and Justice[21] tells us that "virtually all psychopaths have been rejected by at least one parent in early childhood and consequently develop an attitude of mistrust, insensitivity, or hostility toward other human beings, although they may retain an ability to manipulate others for their own goals. Severely rejected children, particularly those burdened with a neural disorder, do not develop a conscience, trust in others, or a willingness to consider the interests of others." This is also true, in part, for sociopaths.

In 1986 the term "adopted child syndrome" was used for the first time as part of a murder defense in the trial of Patrick DeGelleke. David Kirschner, child psychiatrist, and Arthur Sorosky, psychiatrist and adoption expert, used the term to incorporate the following symptoms of psychotic rage: conflict with authority; preoccupation with excessive fantasy; setting fires; pathological lying, stealing, running away from home; learning difficulties and lack of impulse control. While most adoptees exhibit some of these traits as a result of their confusion about heritage, it becomes a serious clinical problem in only a small group, Dr. Kirschner emphasized. He also notes that such behaviors can be found in children who are not adopted, but in adopted children they are unconsciously connected to feelings of rejection and abandonment.

Patrick DeGelleke, who was obsessed with a phoenix bird that rises out of its own ashes, read *The Adventures of Huckleberry Finn* and dreamed of running away, of hiding in the woods and of searching for his natural mother. He was fourteen years old on the morning of September 8, 1984, when he splashed lantern fuel outside his adoptive parents' bedroom door and set the room ablaze, killing them both. He was tried as an adult and found guilty of second degree murder.

Patrick and three brothers had been removed from the custody of their natural mother. Two years later, when he was five, Patrick and his brothers left their foster home to be adopted into the DeGelleke family of Marion, New York. His adoptive parents had already adopted nine year old twin girls a year prior. The sudden creation of such a large family caused a strain which placed the entire family in counseling. Patrick's difficulties at home and at school, however, led his parents to file a petition with Family Court, saying they could not control him and asking the court to intervene. Betty Jean Lifton, writing about the case in the *New York Times*,[22] cites the defense attorney's supposition that it was the filing of the petition and Patrick's fear of being rejected once again, which triggered his psychotic rage. Dr. Kirschner said in an interview, "I believe he was really trying to destroy the adoption system which had upset his life." Lifton concludes that the adoption system should have been on trial with him.

James Fox, professor of Criminal Justice at Northeastern University and co-author of *Mass Murder; America's Growing Menace*,[23] told me in a telephone interview that adoptees are over-represented among serial murderers. Ken Bianchi, "The Hillside Strangler"; David Berkowitz, a.k.a., "Son of Sam"; and Gerald Eugene Stano, who killed thirty-two people in Florida, are among the more notorious adoptees in this group. While there were "a lot more adoptees (among this group) than one would expect," Fox cautions against drawing any cause and effect rationale. "We all suffer rejection in our lives," said Fox. "The cause is the rejection, not the adoption." Adoptees often perceive their surrender as a rejection by their birthmother, despite the fact that many mothers must surrender to prove their love. What sociopaths, such as serial murderers, have in common is an inability to deal with rejection. Some people have better coping mechanisms than others. What can lead to physical killing of a human being in one person, can simply lead another person to be a cold and calculating, bloodthirsty businessman committing business "killings" instead, according to Fox.

This is a grim picture of adoption indeed, yet the majority of adopted people lead normal, healthy and productive lives. It is imperative to bear in mind that many of the psychological difficulties raised in the preceding chapter, from the most minor to the most major, can be reduced by humanizing the process of adoption as we will see in Chapter Six.

Kathleen Silber, M.S.W., the state director of Domestic Adoption at Children's Home Society of California, and co-author of *Dear Birthmother*,[24] agrees. "There is a large number of adopted children who are in therapy and in residential treatment centers all over the country," she says. "Since we know there are problems associated with traditional adoptions, we have to explore new options that will promote better mental health for these children, even if there are people who think these options involve some risk."[25]

3

Birthparents:
Unresolvable Grief

*"The only ghosts, I believe, who creep into this world,
are dead young mothers, returned to see how their children
fare. There is no other inducement great enough to bring the
departed back."*—Sir James Barrie, *The Little White Birds*

*"Did someone say that there would be an end,
An end, Oh, an end, to love and mourning?"*—May Sarton

IDENTIFYING BIRTHPARENTS

When the average person thinks about adoption, he or
she thinks about a childless couple and a homeless baby.
Three people. Where did the homeless waif spring from—the
cabbage patch? The original parents are seldom, if ever,
thought of. Most of us know adoptees and adoptive parents,
but we seldom think that for every adoptee there are two
birthparents. We all know birthparents, as well, although we
may not be aware of it because birthparents are not encouraged to talk about their experience.

"Family formation by adoption is an accepted occur-
rence and can be discussed with family and friends.
Family disruption by means of adoption remains

65

shrouded in secrecy. There are slightly less the number of birthparents as adoptees adjusted to the age factor. But few of us can identify who these women are within our circle of friends. At least one woman in every hundred, perhaps one in fifty, has lost a child to adoption."—Gail Davenport, A.C.S.W., Facilitator, The Birthparent Support Network.[1]

Sorosky, Baran, and Pannor note that "the birth parent has been the mysterious 'hidden' parent around whom the adoptee and adoptive parent have been able to weave positive and negative fantasies."[2]

For years, I drove around with two bumper stickers on my car which read "Root for Adoptees' Rights" and "Adoptees Have Roots and Rights." I was often stopped and asked if I was adopted or if my children were adopted, or my husband. When I answered "no" to all of the above, people were at a loss to imagine why I had such bumper stickers. Never did it occur to any of these people that I was the third side of the triangle, a birthparent. I have often wondered why.

Is it because they think of a woman who gives up a child for adoption as being young and I am mature? Is it because birthmothers are thought of as "bad" girls, and these people were seeing me as I am now: a wife, writer and mother? Is it because birthmothers are thought of as living in secrecy and no one would suspect I would "admit" to having committed such a hideous crime, such an unnatural act, as giving away my own child? Or is it simply that they do not think of us at all? Sorosky, Baran and Pannor found that many prospective adopters have been encouraged *not* to think of birthparents. They describe a 1971 publication by two adoption workers who claimed that "in order to 'reinforce the adoptive parent-child bond' . . . the adoptive parents should be provided with as little information as possible on the 'shadowy figures' of the birth parents."[3]

Susan and Elton Klibanoff further explain this phenomenon. "The person who sets the adoption process in motion is often given very little thought—at least by the adoptive parents. That person is the child's biological mother, usually an unwed mother.

"There are many reasons why she is so overlooked. Some parents want to forget the fact that she ever existed. They consider her irresponsible or worthless. Some are embarrassed by the fact that she is the reason for their having children. Others hope that if she is never mentioned, the children might put off their questions about her. Most have never met a girl in a position of giving up a child, and just don't know what to think about her."[4]

New Zealand author Joss Shawyer agrees: "After ploughing through twenty books, I began to wonder if adopted children had actually had mothers or whether they'd germinated on the window sills of social service departments."[5]

But it need not always be so. In a public hearing before the Assembly Institutions, Health and Welfare Committee on adoption held December 9, 1981 in Trenton, New Jersey, attorney Harold Cassidy told how public attitudes toward birthparents could be changed:

"There is a need for us in society to learn to know the women who have come to call themselves 'birthmothers.' They are women who know that a child is part of his mother forever. They are women who know that separation can never sever the bond between them. They know what it means to love a child and to place the child's welfare above all else in life. They know the pain of wanting what is best for the child they love, while society tells them that what is best is that they never see that child again. They know the ultimate act of love. They know the ultimate sacrifice. They know the never ending grief of being continually denied what every portion of their souls demands: the knowledge that their children are well.

"We, as a society, have perpetrated the cruelest deception. What we have believed to be altruistic has been, in reality, destructive. We have sought to create without any understanding of how much we destroy in the process.

"Birthparents now know that separating a mother

and her child is not in the best interests of either of them. Their enormous sacrifice was based on society's misconceptions. The adoptees' sense of rejection is the most painful irony of all: what was done out of love is mistaken for a lack of it.

"For us to truly learn what a birthparent is, is to learn that we, as a society, are hypocritical. We urge surrender, then later rebuke it. We make laws that we purport to be for the welfare of our children, then ignore or suppress their pleas to satisfy the most fundamental and compelling need they have: to know their mothers.

"What we must understand is that we have held imprisoned an important part of these women. They must be made whole again. This task will not be difficult when we understand who they are.

"They are our mothers.

"They are our sisters.

"They are our daughters."

Who then are birthparents, these nameless, faceless people who begot children they are never allowed to see? Sociologically and statistically, birthmothers have most often been from white, upper-middle or middle class homes, as more single mothers in lower socio-economic groups could opt to keep their babies because they faced considerably less stigma. By and large, birthmothers are not promiscuous, as more sophisticated and experienced women know more about birth control.

"It is our experience, gained from intimate knowledge of practically forty-five hundred cases, that the mothers of these babies are good girls. To some, in the safety of their matrimonial ties, it may seem paradoxical to call these unfortunates 'good girls.' But they are in the majority of cases simple, unsophisticated young girls, lacking knowledge of their sexual self, who either through love or ignorance make their first misstep . . ."
—The Willows catalog.[6]

Some birthmothers are religiously, morally or personally opposed to abortion. Others could not obtain one because

68

they were illegal at the time, too expensive and/or too dangerous.

Most of the birthmothers of today's teenage adoptees were teenagers and often still in high school at the time they became pregnant, often with their first love. In many instances they planned to marry, and might have been officially or unofficially engaged. Many birthmothers remember believing, up until the day they signed the papers, that their children's fathers would come to their rescue and marry them.

Birthfathers are generally teens or young adults, and frightened. A few are married men, often unbeknownst to the birthmother at the time of conception. Some birthfathers are never told of the pregnancy. Others do the "right" thing and agree to, or even insist upon, marrying their girlfriends, but parents often refuse permission if they are underage. Some birthfathers simply deny the child is theirs.

Although a naive young woman becoming pregnant with her first love is perhaps the most common scenario, there are others as well. I have met women who became birthmothers as a result of rape, and who still had thoughts and love for their children and were in fact actively searching for them. Other women were married or divorced and the children were not their husbands'. A surrendered child is most often the birthmother's first or only, but not always. Adoptees could have older siblings, younger siblings, both or neither.

"A teenager dying from an inoperable brain tumor had an emotional reunion yesterday with the woman who gave her up for adoption a few days after she was born. Janine Malone, eighteen, of St. Petersburg, and her natural mother, Donna Hufnagel, of Medford, NY, met at Tampa International Airport. Mrs. Hufnagel, thirty-nine, later married and had three more children."
—Associated Press, Tampa, FL, 25 August, 1986.

GETTING CAUGHT

"Children of the future Age
Reading this indignant page,
Know that in a former time
Love! sweet Love! was thought a crime."
—William Blake

Using the most common scenario, young women from "good" families, often in school, became pregnant out of wedlock. Their parents, as intelligent, caring people, wanting to do what they believed was best for their daughters and their children, which included "saving face," often sent their daughters away to "serve time" in homes for unwed mothers. Expectant young mothers have been sent thousands of miles from home to help keep the family's secret. Many were sent under assumed names to spare the family shame.

"At this point I was alone and in a strange city. My self-esteem was at zero and why wouldn't it be? At the 'home' we were not encouraged to make friends, our last names were scratched off our letters, and nothing was done to make us feel good about ourselves. For years afterward, I felt that anyone who looked at me could see my experience all over my face."—M.S., Syracuse, NY.

Being treated like a prisoner adds to the mothers' feelings of being punished, of having done some awful thing. Accounts of homes for unwed mothers parallel descriptions of prisons, with girls working in the laundry, the kitchen or the nursery.

"She never went back to the ward for the girls, except during the day when they were all in the laundry room, working. everything seemed anticlimactic; the tall thin one she passed in the hall spoke as if she hardly knew her.

where did these girls go after the births of their babies? what wind blew them away like ashes? those she loved well, without question, those she was taught not to believe in, the whore, where did they

go when they were flat and empty, when they fit back
into their old clothes?

like shamed nuns, they left the dormitory, silent.
their clothes were delivered in a paper sack, and
they dressed hurriedly in the dark. the papers had
been signed. most had asked to be blindfolded.
downstairs, in the laundry, creatures like giant
insects continued to hum and move their metal arms
the ones that were left fed them like robots."
—Toi Derricotte, *Natural Birth.*[7]

The inmates' "sentences" do not end when they walk out
the maternity home doors, bellies, arms and hearts empty,
but rather begin.

> ". . . It is a life sentence with no parole. Birth-
> mothers are consigned to a special level of hell, where we
> burn forever in a frozen flame that tortures, but does not
> consume, and gives no light . . . (Adoption) is an institu-
> tionalized form of symbolic infanticide, with all the hor-
> ror, revulsion and guilt intact . . . We feel like murderers
> because we ARE murderers—but we killed with a pen,
> not a gun . . . Adoption does not kill the body, but it
> surely kills a large part of the soul, both of the mother
> and of the child."—Mary Anne Cohen.[8]

This is severe treatment for women whose "crime" was
being in love or being victimized, who neither abused nor
abandoned their children. Beyond the physical similarity,
there are other psychological comparisons that can be drawn
between young women incarcerated during the term of their
pregnancies and criminal inmates. Both are isolated and
limited in their boundaries. Some may get visits, letters or
calls from home, others may not.

> "Without describing painful details, several general
> factors stand out in what happened. One factor was my
> passivity. Never having dealt with a personal crisis
> before, and not being at all experienced in expressing
> myself, my wishes or concerns, I blindly went along with
> authority figures around me. Another factor involved

was the prevailing social attitude toward 'unwed mothers.'

"Being an unwed mother in middle America was essentially the end of one's life and virtually a crime, redeemable only by surrendering your baby, and pretending it didn't happen . . .

"Although the agency involved was a reputable one, I was never told anything about any of my rights or any alternatives to adoption or anything about procedures or even childbirth itself. I was shuffled around like a prisoner and felt and acted like one. Fantasies about escape always ended up with images of me and my baby lying in a gutter starving somewhere."—Robin L. Wilson.[9]

America has the highest teen pregnancy rate in the industrial world. 1.1 million teenage girls—three out of ten—become pregnant each year in this country. Approximately forty percent opt for abortion. Of those carrying the baby to term, ninety-five percent keep their babies, according to 1982 data.[10] Because there are fewer women today considering adoption, many homes for unwed mothers have been closed. Those which choose to remain open, or some which have recently opened, are a new breed of more aggressive, hard-sell homes. Arty Elgart—who has been called "Mr. Stork" by CBS television on "60 Minutes"—and his unorthodox adoption agency, the Golden Cradle, is one example of what is currently happening to replace former maternity homes, substituting a "home to live in during the term of your pregnancy. A home that is more than a shelter. A home that surrounds you with the warmth and understanding that can only come from people who share your concern for the life you carry." So reads the brochure of the Golden Cradle, one of the country's five largest agencies placing healthy American infants with adoptive couples. "Though the couple that you stay with will not be the couple who adopt your child," the brochure continues, "you will have an opportunity to share this most important time with two people who have met our most thorough selection requirements for adopting parents."[11]

The couples with whom the pregnant women are placed

are indeed concerned about the lives they are carrying, but perhaps have a less vested interest in the carriers. While Elgart never allows the prospective parents of a particular woman's child to house that same woman, the thorough selection requirements of which he speaks include requiring that each set of prospective parents house an expectant mother for someone else. Each couple knows that the better job they do of convincing the current resident in their home to surrender, the better chance they have to get the next baby on the list. There is a grave potential here, which is in need of investigation, of the resident expectant mothers developing "Stockholm Syndrome," in which hostages identify with their captors. Elgart, a former physical education teacher and owner of a wholesale auto parts warehouse, has no formal training in the field of adoption. He has been called aggressive, charming, demanding, dedicated, charismatic and something of a cult figure by the *Philadelphia Inquirer*.[12] Louis M. Natali, former first assistant defender of Philadelphia, was quoted in August, 1983 in the *Philadelphia Inquirer* as being convinced that there have been enough complaints about Golden Cradle to warrant it being "looked at seriously" by authorities. Natali claimed that the agency makes birthmothers feel "like they owe their babies to Golden Cradle . . ."

Some birthmothers never go to any type of "home" during their pregnancies. Some stay home, often denying their pregnancies until well past the first trimester; till "quickening," or the feeling of life. Still others confided in their parents, seeking help, and were met with their parents' way of trying to deny the truth:

> "My parents, when it was apparent to them that my child would not have a father, were greatly upset and, fearing embarrassment, confined me to my room for the duration of my pregnancy, during which period I had no prenatal care, not for lack of funds on the part of my parents, but because they were ashamed and feared that relatives not of the immediate family, friends or neighbors might become aware of my condition. I was permitted to leave my room only when my father was not

at home or when both my parents would be out or away on a trip—usually for a weekend. I was never allowed to go outdoors, even on the front porch, at any time." —S.R.C., Belmar, NJ.

"I became pregnant when I was seventeen. My upper middle-class family told friends that I was in an auto accident. They kept me confined to the house and I was locked in the closet any time anyone came to visit. That was in 1967."—B.K., Fairfield, IA.

Dr. Deykin, assistant professor at Harvard University School of Public Health, studied 334 birthparents and found that sixty-nine percent "cited external factors, such as family opposition and pressure from social workers, as the primary reason for surrender."[13] There are others who have a role in shaping these women's futures other than their boyfriends and their parents. In most instances social workers become involved if the parents elect to work through an agency. Otherwise, parents may opt to handle it all privately through an attorney or a doctor and attorney team. Such private arrangements may vary in shades from grey to black market. While "many lawyers specializing in adoption act ethically and responsibly . . . some, in effect, serve as little more than brokers at an infant auction."[17]

"Mine was a private adoption arranged by my physician. I was registered in the hospital under a false name. Today my medical records and my daughter's are all missing and our patient numbers are registered to old men."—B.K., Fairfield, IA.

The preferred way is through a legitimate private, religious or public adoption agency which will screen prospective adoptive parents for more attributes than their ability to pay. Here, too, the parents can delegate the job of persuading their daughter to do the "right" thing. Here someone else can help persuade her to come to her senses and do what is "best."

COUNSELING

Mary Benet, author of *Politics of Adoption*, states that "Relinquishing a baby for adoption is an index of the pressures in society."

Joss Shawyer finds the same is true of adoptions in New Zealand: "Where 'counseling' was provided most of the babies were adopted—obviously a direct result of the 'counseling' provided . . ." She further states that the few single mothers who survived pregnancy with their babies wore wedding rings and invented "ficticious, legitimately-absent husbands" such as sailors. Adoption was never mentioned to them, says Shawyer, who believes that lawsuits would ensue if they said to married women the same things told to the unwed. On the other hand, "you'd be amazed," Shawyer states, "how stubborn some women can be. They fight hard against adoption and even insist that they want this child. The social worker quite naturally gets very cross when confronted by such an 'unrealistic' woman. A lot of energy is spent getting 'unrealistic' women to see that they can't possibly care for this baby . . ."[14]

This fact is exemplified here in the United States by studies such as the recently completed study of ninety-two agencies and one hundred and thirty-two pregnancy counselors in Illinois serving approximately 19,000 pregnant adolescents in 1982, which revealed the following: for those counselors who promoted adoption, thirty-six percent of their clients chose adoption, for all other groups the surrender rate was only two percent.[15]

At agencies such as the Edna Gladney Home of Texas, ninety percent of the residents surrender; while in charitable residences for unwed mothers, like Kathy DiFiore's Several Sources Foundation, Ramsey, New Jersey, ninety percent of the unpressured women choose to keep their babies.

Reuben Pannor, social worker and co-author of *The Adoption Triangle*, confirms, "They shyly sought help, but instead, someone badgered into them the idea that they'd done something terrible and they felt they had to be punished for it."

The counseling most expectant mothers receive is done

by workers at the agency handling the placement of the child —workers whose livelihoods depend on placing children. In any other area of life, this would clearly be seen as conflict of interest. While adoptive parents almost always have an attorney present to represent them, the relinquishing parent is rarely, if ever, advised to seek legal counsel while she signs an irrevocable waiver of her rights. No legal counsel while she signs her name to a piece of paper that will affect her for the rest of her life, her child for the rest of his or her life, as well as both of their families. In many states a minor can sign relinquishment of her child. Furthermore, many birthmothers are not given a copy of what they've signed, and some, like myself, still can get no copy of it years later. There are no other legal contracts which the parties signing cannot obtain.

ANONYMITY

No discussion of adoption records to adult adoptees is free from references regarding the "right" of the birthmother to anonymity and confidentiality. The protection of the birthmother's "new life" is perhaps the most often cited reason for keeping adoption records sealed, yet ironically anonymity may be something which in most cases, the birthmother has never requested.

Whenever you hear this concern raised, take note as to who is raising it. More often than not, because birthparents have not been encouraged to speak, it is not a birthparent, or a group which represents birthparents, which is voicing this concern. William Pierce, president of the National Committee for Adoption, for instance, has been quoted as saying: ". . . women place their children for adoption with the guarantee of lifelong confidentiality . . ."[16] This is in direct contradiction to the facts as known to the authorities in the field:

"From the data being reported . . . there is good reason to believe that when they surrendered their children, few mothers understood the full meaning of the confidentiality agencies now say they implicitly promised them. Are agencies forcing on these mothers the 'right' to a confidentiality they never intended to have and may not wish to maintain with respect to their children?"[17]

"My experience has shown that birthparents are able to release children for adoption with the knowledge that the law might change at some future date . . . It is my opinion that we should not assume that all birthparents want the confidentiality they were promised."[18]

"Having talked with many birthparents in recent months, I have come to believe, first, that the birthparents were not interested in perpetual anonymity but rather, that we, the agency representatives, have thought they were interested in this, due to the stigma attached in past years to the out-of-wedlock pregnancy."[19]

"The secrecy of the sealed record was to hide their shame. What it did, instead, was to intensify it by making birthmothers feel they'd done something so hideous that all reference to it had to be locked away and never reopened."[20]

It is also interesting that in many agency adoptions, the confidentiality which is promised to all parties in the adoption often turns out to be quite one-sided. In many adoptions, the adoptive parents receive a copy of the adoption decree, which often contains the child's original first and last name, and sometimes the mother's first name as well. Could this be because, according to Delores M. Schmidt, Director of Family and Aging Services, Catholic Services, Denver, Colorado, "confidentiality protected his adoptive parents from publicly facing the reality of their childlessness."[21] The purpose of maintaining sealed records has most widely been attributed to protecting the parties involved from "outsiders." They serve instead to sever the parties from each other.

Further verification of this new light on the issue of birthparents' anonymity is seen in the percentages of birthparents contacted at random by their adopted-out offspring. Groups such as ALMA (Adoptees Liberty Movement Association) and others are seeing a ninety percent or better "success" rate of birthparents accepting a child who finds them. Their findings serve only to validate the findings of Sorosky, Baran and Pannor, authors of *The Adoption Triangle,* who found that eighty-five percent of birthparents interviewed were curious about their surrendered child and, though many would not initiate a search, most would not turn away a child who found them.

Gail Davenport, M.S.W., A.C.S.W., believes that the counseling many birthmothers receive is in direct opposition to all commonly held practices of therapy. Davenport calls it "pregnancy counseling" which is focused only upon the pregnancy and not with any discussion of the baby beyond infancy. In most forms of therapeutic counseling, clients are helped through option exploration to see the short and long term effects of their actions. Not so in counseling unwed mothers. Other forms of psychotherapy and analysis emphasize the positive, possibly pointing out that in five years children are less dependent and in school. Not so in adoption counseling. Young, pregnant women sit before counselors at one of the most vulnerable times in their lives, a time of intense crisis. Psychologically, pregnancy and the post-partum period, even under the best of circumstances, with a loving and supportive mate, is an emotionally unstable time. Mood swings are a common phenomenon at this time. Add to this isolation, desertion by lover and/or family, and feelings of guilt for having done something shameful and awful.

By virtue of gender, age and financial dependence, single mothers are rendered powerless and vulnerable to decisions made on their behalf. They are often alone and frightened, hoping that their Knight in Shining Armor will come to their rescue. Hoping for a miracle.

"There is a gaping hole and unrelenting ache in my heart since the day I relinquished my son. His father and I loved each other, we wanted him, planned for him and looked forward to his arrival. Unfortunately, four months before his arrival, circumstances too complicated to go into necessitated our separation. It was my mother's decision that I surrender my child—her influence was overpowering. I didn't sign final papers until my son was six months old, hoping and praying with all my might that some miracle would make it possible for me to awaken from this nightmare and find my baby in my arms.''—G.P. Canton, SD.

Too frequently birthparents are not offered suggestions as to how to get a job. Are they told about day-care centers? Are they informed of their legal rights, that a young woman is an emancipated minor once she becomes pregnant? Are services such as public assistance made known to them? Are they asked, as they would be in any other type of counseling situation, what they want to do? Are birthfathers told of their right to parent? All too often, they are not. Instead of being helped to explore alternatives, they are attacked at their most vulnerable points, thus magnifying inadequacies rather than putting them into proper perspective. "Yes, that's right," they are often told, "You have no job and babies cost a great deal of money. You wouldn't want to make your baby suffer, would you?"

Expectant parents' instinctive desire to provide what is best for their children is thus used as a tool against them. Young people who consistently hear from their parents and other authority figures that their children need "better" and to relinquish is "best," begin to assume that they are "no good" for their own children, that they are not fit parents.

Even if the expectant mothers and/or fathers are college students or graduates and/or have visible means of support, it is pointed out that keeping their children at this point in time would ruin their lives and that they might eventually resent their children and thus risk becoming abusive parents.

At the Annual Conference of American Orthopsychiatric Association in 1974, Annette Baron, M.S.W., told of her years working for adoption agencies. "Over the past fifteen years I have seen many birthparents who should never have relinquished their children and would not have if they had really been given the right to decide, and not made to feel guilty if they kept, and I have to admit that I was probably instrumental in perpetuating this practice for a long time."

Dr. Samuel Roll, professor of psychology and psychiatry at the University of New Mexico, studying birthmothers, concurs. He found the women he worked with "didn't give up their babies of their own free will. 'Of your own will' means that you've had a chance to explore your ambivalence, to openly explore what the opportunities are and what they all cost. None of these women had that experience."[22]

Under any other circumstances, family counseling would be in order. The pregnancies of unmarried women affect their extended families. Such family members are a valuable resource and need to be consulted to explore their desires and capabilities in terms of parenting their grandchildren, nieces, nephews, cousins, etc. Instead of explaining to the prospective grandparents, for instance, the permanency of the loss of their grandchildren, parents and their expectant daughters are often counseled separately, neither knowing until it is too late that they were not, as they had thought, doing what the other had wished.

> "The social worker never spoke to us all together. My parents were in one room and I was in another. At home, we never spoke about it, each thinking the other was doing what they wanted. Now my parents feel that they were ill-informed and received inadequate counseling."
> —Susan Russell, Angles and Extensions, Roswell, Georgia.

> "I dreamed of arranging foster care for my little one while I pressed my parents to accept us both back into the family until I could finish high school. (I never knew until recently that my mother would have agreed to such a plan.) No one ever sat us all down together and I was too demoralized and withdrawn to insist on such a discussion."—Robin L. Wilson, Durham, NC.[23]

> "When I tried to speak with the workers at the agency my daughter had contacted, they treated me as if I

were infringing on her privacy rather than fighting for the rights of MY grandchild."—Deborah Green, Philadelphia, PA.

Still alone, in most instances, their pregnancies culminate with labor and delivery, an event for which most surrendering mothers are ill-prepared, or not prepared at all. In one clinical study of women who had surrendered children to adoption, Dr. Rynearson found that "all of the women had dreaded delivery. They remember labor as a time of loneliness and painful panic."[24] Many cherish the time while they can feel and "talk to" their babies in their wombs and fear the onset of labor, knowing it represents, for them, a loss. "During this time," Rynearson found, "the subjects established an intense private monologue with the fetus, including a rescue fantasy in which they and the newborn infant would somehow be 'saved' from the relinquishment." Many birthmothers give birth alone and frightened with no support person and must keep silent a psychological and physiological event in their lives which other women are allowed to celebrate joyously.

Birthparents' families and society have set the foundation for feelings of self-doubt and worthlessness. While trying to rid young women of a "burden" that might ruin their lives, they have replaced it with a much larger handicap.

"Seven years ago—I was sixteen—I gave up my infant daughter to Social Services. I went to stay with friends. The boy was seventeen and we've remained friends to this day. I was never offered any other alternative whatsoever. I feel the social worker had more interest in obtaining my baby for a 'deserving' couple than in helping me."—J.C.D., Cincinnati, OH.

THEN AND NOW

I am often confronted with the argument that "That was then. Things like that don't happen now." Many adoption social workers have told me that "girls are counseled differently today than they were years ago." This is true in some states, in some agencies, and of some social workers. Unfortunately, it is not as yet universally true, as evidenced by the court battle between Barbara Landry and the Edna Gladney Home of Fort Worth, Texas in April, 1984.

Barbara was a single, working girl of nineteen who became pregnant while living at home in the Bronx, New York. Her boyfriend suggested abortion, which she could not go through with. She then found the Edna Gladney Home through a listing in a New York telephone book. They paid her expenses to Texas and housed and fed her during her pregnancy. They helped her to fabricate a story to her parents that she was working in Florida. Barbara said in a number of interviews that all of the counseling she received at the home was geared towards how wonderful adoption would be. She said that she and other residents at the home were shown films and were introduced to couples who were eager to adopt children, and to some couples who already had. On the "Phil Donahue Show," on which Barbara appeared, a representative of the Gladney Home repeated twice that girls like Barbara, if they do keep their babies, "wind up living with some guy who will abuse their babies," as if this were their only alternative.

Barbara signed a surrender when her baby was four days old, under a great deal of stress and confusion, she says. When Barbara's family learned the truth of her situation, they rushed to Texas to support her. When Barbara's son was two days old, her parents told the agency not to place him in an adoptive home. Barbara officially changed her mind ten days after signing the surrender, deciding that she really wanted to keep her baby. In her custody battle, which she lost, Barbara was forced to prove herself a fit mother. How ironic that with one stroke of the pen one is accused of being unfit for doing exactly what she was told was the best thing for her baby!

There are other ironies. In Texas, for instance, a birth-mother's surrender, once signed, is irrevocable. This is done for the good of the baby, who would be psychologically damaged by being placed and then removed from a place-

82

ment. Barbara's baby at the time of the court proceedings was only two months old. Many premature babies are separated from their mothers for more than two months. Yet in the same state, Texas, adoptive parents have six months to change their minds. Similar laws exist in most states. Whom do they protect?

Women such as Landry are in exile from their families, either voluntary or mandatory. They are financially dependent on their keepers. Many women, such as Landry, are told that if they renege on their promise to surrender they will have to pay all medical, legal, food and board expenses. This is clearly emotional blackmail. Women's vulnerability at this time is often used to "make them see the light" just as many religious cults do.

The difference between today and yesterday is that fewer young women carry an unplanned pregnancy to term today. Of those who do, many have the option today of raising their children as single parents. The small percentage who still consider adoption have the option of making private arrangements. An unmarried expectant mother of today who has supportive parents, or financial independence, can visit a private physician and will not be pressured in any way to surrender. It is the small percentage of such women who seek help through religious or state agencies who find that the pressure to surrender is just as great, if not greater, than ever before. Because of dwindling supply and increasing demand, white, healthy infants are more in demand now than ever before.

Prior to 1986 it would have been unheard of for a song such as Madonna's "Papa Don't Preach" with lyrics that shout: "I'm keeping my baby!" to be number one. Times have certainly changed, and with them many attitudes toward women's roles and parenting. But Barbara Landry is only one case which made headlines. She is representative of many women caught in the "baby wanted" eighties.

Another woman told me that in 1987 she sought the help of twenty-two lawyers before finding one who would agree to take her case of attempting to overturn a relinquishment.

If one can understand and have compassion for the parents of birthmothers, who in most cases have the well-being of their children (and their children's children) in their hearts, one can only speculate about the motive of social workers and agencies. They, too, are often victims of the myths surrounding single mothers. They believe that what they are doing is best for the mothers as well as the babies because, they rationalize, the "girls" are young and can always have other children.

The former head social worker of a New York adoption agency, now retired, explains: "We, as social workers, were trained to believe, not always to feel, that in some way we were doing these women justice by not allowing them to suffer at the hands of the world. The world is judgmental, but then so were we, I realize. I am able to look back and see my error of judgment especially during those times I performed my job 'adequately.' How often I had to tell a young, inexperienced biological mother that she would forget her child and should be grateful for the opportunity to start a 'new life.' Did I believe this? I don't know . . . the majority of the biological mothers were those who were young, frightened and wanting desperately for someone to do something or say something which could change the decision which remained to be made. Yes, many did want to keep their children, but society was not prepared to handle that decision then, without negative consequences to the mother and the child . . ."[25]

One myth that must be shattered is that surrendering parents can have other children someday. This may not always be the case. Kathleen Sly, of Concerned United Birthparents, told a *Los Angeles Times* reporter "CUB sort of breaks into two groups. Half the members have had no other children because the pain is so great. The other group has had one child after another. We were told we could replace the child we surrendered. I have three, and it didn't replace my son."

> "Every time I look at a photograph of my family, it's as if someone's missing." Mary Anne Cohen, Whippany, NJ.

Those, like myself, who are blessed with subsequent children, have a daily reminder of what we missed while those who have no other children suffer a different, though surely no lesser pain. Some defer childbearing because of a conscious or subconscious fear that God will punish them. Some fear insulting the memory of their lost child. Some fear re-living the birth experience. Some have tried unsuccessfully and have suffered secondary infertility or miscarriages.

"I cannot deny the gnawing anxiety that fills me at the thought of actually being pregnant. In past times—those numb days—my eyes averted all swollen bellies . . . endless years of denial . . . normal excuses . . . moved . . . tests . . . I have come to realize that I am trying to fulfill the agency's criteria for parental eligibility . . . Pregnancy is an obscene condition, a state to be shunned, scorned . . . The ultimate betrayal of myself, the extraction of my flesh."—Susan Russell, ORIGINS Newsletter, May/June, 1986.

A survey of three hundred and thirty-four members of Concerned United Birthparents indicates that birthparents have a disproportionately high rate of secondary infertility as compared to the general populace. Of the three hundred and thirty-four surveyed, three hundred and eight provided information on their subsequent fertility and reproductive attempts. Of those, two hundred and eight, or sixty-four percent, had been successful in having at least one live-born child following the surrender; forty-five subjects (fourteen percent) reported that they had tried but had been unable to produce another child; and fifty-five respondents (seventeen percent) stated that they had chosen to remain childless. Eliminating those who chose not to have subsequent children, the rate of secondary infertility among this sample is 16.2%. This rate is significantly higher—170% higher—than the six percent general population rate of secondary infertility among couples who have one child and desire another. The rate is also higher than the fifteen percent rate of primary infertility for the U.S.[26] Such statistics are staggering, but the reality is even more harsh.

"I am an adoptive mother of six beautiful children. Three were adopted as older children and three as infants. I am also a birthmother. I lost my daughter to adoption seventeen years ago . . . believe me when I say I understand the pain of infertility and the burning desire to hold a baby in your arms and call it your own . . . I have been pregnant eight times, and only the first pregnancy came to term, and she is the child I surrendered to adoption. Not once in my eight pregnancies did I take for granted the life I had created."—Theresa, California, CUB Communicator, December, 1984.

It is not known whether the disproportion has a psychosomatic basis or not, but contrary to the problem stated in the book, *Ended Beginnings*,[27] that birthmothers may experience difficult subsequent births, many women who surrender a child to adoption have been unsuccessful in subsequent attempts to conceive or to carry another pregnancy to term. Others have never married, while still others have had to have hysterectomies for medical reasons after surrendering their only child to adoption. All have been left childless mothers.

Childless Mother
Standing by,
Hearing all
Society's cry!

"Poor, poor dear
Never to know
The warm feeling
Of nature's glow"
—Susan Russell[28]

Counseling of pregnant women in crisis must be honest in reflecting both the unresolvable nature of surrender and the fact that the surrendered child might be the only child the man or woman will ever have.

"The part that always bugged me the most was when the girls in the office would complain about their spreading hips and blame it on childbirth. Then they'd look at me in my size fives and say: 'Oh, Jan, you're so lucky you never were pregnant.' They should only know that I gave up TWO kids!'"—J.B., W. Long Branch, NJ.

"It has taken a good many lonely years of having to say 'no' to the question 'Do you have any children of your own?' Wanting, every time to scream to the world, 'Yes, I have a son!' years of silence . . ."—Georgie Hayward, NJ.

SHORT TERM EFFECTS

Some birthparents are convinced that surrendering their children to adoption was "right" and "best." For many, it is the only way to survive, at least temporarily, the physical and emotional ripping away of a part of themselves. Some are "brainwashed" to leave the process feeling somehow virtuous and self-sacrificing. I know, I did. But I also felt empty and as if I had nothing left to live for. Mostly there was, for me, as for many, a numbness. I worked hard at keeping my senses numb.

Some are made to feel noble and proud of what they've done. I have heard such birthmothers shortly after surrendering, dutifully saying: "I-did-the-right-thing. I-am-glad-I-gave-my-baby-up. My-baby-will-have-a-better-home-than-I-could-ever-have-given-it. And-I've-made-a-childless-couple-happy."

Many birthmothers spend their lives convincing themselves that they were right. They must, for to admit otherwise would shatter their image of themselves. For some women, convincing themselves that what they did was right is so important that their lives become shaped by justification. I remember a birthmother/social worker who attended a birthmothers' meeting and told us of her work with adoption placements and her great empathy for adoptive parents. Thus, she, and others, daily justify their actions.

Others come to realize in time that they were victimized into submission and that it is not "right" or natural or normal for a woman to give up her own flesh and blood. Those who speak so positively about surrendering are seldom, if ever, those who have had a great many years to reflect on

87

what has happened because with time comes a growing realization of the tremendous loss suffered. Some are shocked into reality when they decide to share their noble deed with a friend. Instead of being applauded for having done what they were told was "right," they are asked, "How could you?" in horror, disbelief and disdain. "How could you give away your own baby?" Suddenly, or perhaps slowly, many birthparents realize that they have been duped.

I am often asked how this could have happened. I remember reading an analogy written by Lee Campbell, former President of CUB, comparing women who surrender children to adoption to Jews being led to slaughter in Nazi Germany during World War II. How could so few soldiers have annihilated an entire race of people? Why didn't they rebel? The answer, for the Jews and for birthmothers, is that they felt it was hopeless.

VIET NAM VETS AND BIRTHMOTHERS

Viet Nam vets and birthmothers. What could they possibly have in common? A lot!

The vets were young at the time, seventeen, eighteen, nineteen, twenty. Birthmothers are generally young, too.

They were faced with a war—something no one wants or asks for. We were faced with unplanned pregnancies.

They describe themselves now as having been naive. Most didn't even think about what they were getting into. Besides, their alternatives were bleak—leave the country?

Many of us were given no alternatives at all—give up your baby or don't come home.

They went on what they believed to be a noble mission—defending their country. To counteract the fact that killing and maiming are against human nature, they were told that they were killing in the name of peace, freedom and the American way.

We were told that if we really loved our babies and wanted what was best for them, we would give them up

88

to people who could provide better homes for them than we could. Though it is against every act of nature and a violation of our inborn maternal instinct to give away that which we carried and nourished inside our wombs for nearly a year—we were told not to was selfish.

If they refused to go they were called cowards, draft dodgers. They would have been ridiculed by their countrymen, permanently black-balled and possibly even jailed. Had we refused to surrender, we would have been called selfish and unfit parents. Many would have been disowned by our families and/or possibly have had our parental rights severed by the courts.

So they went. They did the noble thing.

We surrendered. We did the "right" thing.

They returned to find less than a hero's welcome. Far from saviours, they were called killers by many. We are not applauded for our sacrifice either, but looked upon with scorn and disgust by friends and neighbors.

They can never put their experience behind them; some experience flashbacks. Like them, we can never forget; we experience anniversary reaction and delayed grief syndrome.

Like them, no one can truly understand our suffering except another who has lived through it. Like them, we are now ready to come out of our closets and make the world understand us.

They are the men of the sixties. We are the women of the sixties . . . and the seventies and the eighties. Their war is over. Ours still rages on.

—Marsha Riben, 1983.

LIVING LIES

Birthparents learn to deal with their loss in various ways. The ways depend upon the makeup of the individual, his or her strengths and weaknesses, life situations, the amount of support or lack of it from family and friends, and the circumstances surrounding the painful situation. Psychologists agree that the more control one has over decisions, the easier it is to accept and deal with them. With a decision as important and irrevocable as surrender, the more pressured the surrendering parents feel, the more resentment they will harbor later.

The traditional states of mourning a loss are: shock, denial, depression, anger, acceptance and resolution. In adoption loss there is no finality as there is with death; thus, no resolution. Anne Brodzinsky, who has studied adoption with her husband, David Brodzinsky, at Rutgers University, New Jersey, has "mapped" the grief of birthmothers based on models of Bolby, Lifton and Lindeman:

EARLY GRIEF
shock and numbing
alarm and retreat
denial and disbelief

ACUTE GRIEF
realization
yearning and pining—searching—desire to
    retrieve what has been lost
anger, guilt and shame—loss of self-esteem
disorganization
reorganization—critical turning point—
    ordering the facts surrounding the loss

SUBSIDING GRIEF
restoration of self-esteem
enhancement of self-esteem
subsiding of acute pain
caring for others and self
looking to the future
animation of grief—publicly or privately
self-help groups
public speaking
sharing

Because there is no resolution, birthmothers may appear to exhibit pathological, as opposed to normal, bereavement.

Dr. Edward Rynearson, who studied birthmothers in a clinical setting in Seattle, Washington, confirms that "the loss is irreversible because the child continues to live." The particular limbo-loss birthparents experience has been aptly labeled "unresolvable grief" by Rynearson. While many birthparents use denial as a coping mechanism, others face a great deal of depression, and others still have turned the rage outward into anger as the following two birthparent poems exemplify:

PREREUNION PAIN

I am filled with hate:
a black, hot cancer of hate
I hide with a hearty grimace
I call a smile
while it consumes me.

I hate the evil agencies
that say nature is nothing
and mothers even less,
that claim to create
while they maim and destroy.

I hate those men of God
who use youthful faith as a sword
to sever hearts and souls,
who promise forgiveness
at the price of martyred lives.

I hate the grasping couples
who pray to God to bless them
by damning families He made,
who self-righteously build greedy joy
on the bodies of bleeding mothers.

I hate the foolish girl I was, who so despised
    herself
she believed she was unworthy,
whose choiceless trust in others' wisdom
made her child a sold commodity.
I am filled with hate
for the agonies of adoption:
its endless, aching injustice,

its everlasting spiritual torment,
and the festering of eternal emptiness.

—C.J. Anderson[29]

ADOPTION SICKNESS

I wish the word "adoption"
were just a word, again, to me—commonplace,
like "chair," or "sink"—
a thing, an object

Devoid
of emotion, or shades of meaning.
Or, more exactly, I wish
The word "adoption" were a concept
so abstract, so ephemeral, like
"Transubstantiation," or "Relativity" . . .

That it could not wound, or stain, or
work its poison into every
corner of my life—
A curiosity, a game for the mind . . .

I wish
The word "Adoption"
were to me what it is to most people—
someone else's problem, from which
most people
turn away . . .

From which I wish I could turn,
could run, could hide,
could erase the word
"Adoption"
From my personal vocabulary
of pain.

—Mary Anne Cohen, Co-Founder, ORIGINS

Rynearson also found that "the relatively immature
defenses of denial, fantasy, and repression appear to have
been the most common defensive responses to the stress of

92

relinquishment." For many, lying to the point of believing the lie becomes a way of life; "blocking out" or repressing, a way to survive the pain. But inside, every denial digs the knife deeper. Many birthparents who have since come to grips with their loss, have reflected back on the years of repression and realized some of the ways it "flashed back" and affected their lives, often without conscious realization.

"I guess like all birthmothers I spent the first six years or so pretending it did not happen, by keeping the reality of her birth buried deep within me, by trying to accept what all the social workers had told me—that years would erase the pain. Then finally I came to the realization that my pain, anger, loss, guilt, and all the other emotional trauma that I was going through were very real, and in no way lessening as time went on."—J.P., Brooklyn, NY.

The pain often does not go away, nor do birthparents forget. Karen Ann Quinlan, whose death after ten years in a coma was well publicized, caused many who had surrendered girls of that age to wonder if it were their child. Many birthparents who surrendered a son the same age as David Berkowitz, the convicted "Son of Sam" murderer prayed he was not their son. Kitty and Peter Carruthers, Olympic team ice skaters, made many a birthparent hope. Every day, in every newspaper, heroes and heroines, criminals and victims, are identified as being the "adopted son of . . ." tearing deeply into the heart of birthparents who have not searched for and found their surrendered children. Constant reminders that strike at men and women, even those who are succeeding with different degrees of "blocking it out."

For others, there is no protective cover-up, no blocking the daily pain. There are birthparents who never "forget" from the instant they give birth, while they sign the dreaded papers, and for every day of the rest of their lives there is not a moment's peace.

"I have a ten and a half year old son whom I was forced to surrender, given none of the alternatives of girls today. I have lived with the agony ever since. There has

93

not been a moment that he has been out of my heart and my mind . . . I've had no one to talk to. My husband is uneasy about it all. My family has erased it from their memories."—C.Z., Baltimore, MD.

Birthparents almost universally report experiencing depression on their children's birthday, or the anniversary of the surrender, or both. For others not a day goes by without a thought or a tear for their lost children. All live with pain, shame and guilt. It's no wonder that many choose to pretend it never happened for fear that others will ostracize them. They have watched themselves anonymously maligned on soap operas and every series from "Little House on the Prairie" to "Dallas."

One birthmother I know of was in group therapy for ten years sharing every inner secret—every one except the fact that she and her husband had a child born to them prior to their marriage who was surrendered for adoption; so strong was her conviction that this was one thing that no one could or would accept.

No matter what external heights of achievement birthparents achieve in life, a seed of self-hate often remains. What would people think if they knew? Who can look at oneself with pride, no matter what status one achieves, with such an ugly skeleton in the closet? Is it any wonder many willingly accept vows of silence?

While birthparents can be expected to keep silent, they should not be expected to forget. When a child is lost to death the parents are consoled, allowed and encouraged to grieve. Birthparents have no grave to bring flowers to. No one sends them condolence cards, and yet neither do birthparents send birth announcements and celebrate.

"I feel that adoption attempts to abort the natural mother instead of the baby."—D.J., British Columbia.

Others have described it as an amputation, while a prolific adoptee called adoption "ancestorcide." And why not? Young, single mothers are often expected to return to school after surrendering their babies, and are told to "act as if nothing happened."

"I remember my mother saying right after the papers were signed in the lawyer's office, 'Well, it's all over now. Let's go out to eat.' I never said anything, but I remember thinking, 'It may be all over for you, but it's just starting for me.' Before, at least I still had her inside me. Now she was gone."—J.T., Staten Island, NY.

COMING OUT

Birthparents are the last, as a group, to come forward and make a place for themselves in the adoption reform movement. Adoptees' groups, such as Orphan Voyage[30] and ALMA[31] had been in existence many years before organizations such as Concerned United Birthparents, Inc., (CUB) helped to raise the consciousness level of many other birthparents in similar circumstances throughout the country.

"My search began in March of this year when a good friend found her birthmother. It was then that I discovered that maybe I too might have a chance. Before then and the 'Phil Donahue Show' on birthparents, I had no idea that CUB, ALMA or anything else existed. I was told when my daughter was born almost sixteen years ago 'forget it, you'll have other children, this is the best for you and her' ad nauseum."—R.V., Raleigh, NC.

Concerned United Birthparents rapidly grew into a national support group for birthparents with thousands of members and local groups in dozens of cities and states. CUB and other similar organizations gave birthparents all over the country the opportunity, for the first time, to speak out and know that they were not the only ones isolated by their secret. Many had never told a living soul about the children they bore. Some pretended their children had died. Some could not remember the date and/or place of birth even when they tried.

"Mine was a private adoption. I saw their name and the license of their car when they drove off with my son. But everyone told me to forget. When I first joined Origins I couldn't remember the name. I had tried. I had combed phone books. Being with the group relaxed me to the point where the name came back to me."—Diane LaMason, Parsippany, NJ.

Others thought they were the only ones who could not forget as they had been told to do by the agency. What solace and comfort to discover that there are approximately twelve million birthparents, many who feel similarly. Dr. Deykin believes that joining a peer self-help group is the first step in resolving the surrender by rejecting denial and secrecy and accepting one's self and acknowledging the birth experience.

"When the meeting began I was the first to introduce myself. 'I am Georgie, and I gave up my son for adoption over twenty-three years ago in Boston.' I don't remember what else I said. It was out, tears in my eyes, but I had finally said it, out loud, for all to hear. It was real, 'My son!' . . . I was finally able to say in front of a large group of people 'I have a son' and not be ashamed of the fact, for the first time in twenty-three years. I was actually able to show Billy's picture to people who truly understood—for they are in my shoes, they can see and feel what I felt and feel, maybe in different degrees and in different ways, but they have been there, they are there, they know. I now, after too many years, realized I am not alone. I was never alone and did not know it till now."—Georgie Hayward, NJ.[32]

The birthparents' movement is in its infancy, even as compared to the adoption reform movement. Every time an article appears in a national magazine, hundreds of letters, such as this one from D.G., Kenai, Alaska, are received:

"Thank you for including the adoption article in your twenty-sixth edition.[33] It provided a catharsis I never thought possible. I read and cried, and wiped and read some more.

"Seventeen years ago I sacrificed my baby to adoption and through your article I glimpsed the obscure possibility that maybe, just maybe, she was not gone from my life forever. That maybe she is curious about me, as I am about her. That maybe she longs to know me, as I long to know her. That maybe by signing the release for adoption I didn't sign away my right to be interested in and concerned about her. Upon reading your article I began 'coming out of the closet.'

"Breaking the secrecy of so many years is a painful process. Emotions deeply supressed in order to hide my 'dirty little secret,' my illegitimate pregnancy and birth, demanded expression and release. For the first time I've indulged and shared my grief over the loss of my baby. By abandoning the secrecy I've finally accepted responsibility for my past, no longer denying the existence of a daughter I so want to be a part of my future. My search has begun and I thank you for providing the impetus."

And from M.S., Kailua, Hawaii:

"You personally are responsible for my awakening and I can't thank you enough. Considering my education and my interests there is no excuse for my ignorance of the adoption situation. I must have been blocking information that came my way. But your article hit me squarely. Since then I read everything I can get my hands on . . ."

Are birthmothers who join groups unique, or are they merely the ones who have heard of such organizations? Every day more and more women are "awakening" and being released from prisons of fear and lies, self-doubt, feelings of worthlessness and self-incrimination. CUB, ORIGINS, and other such organizations which support birthparents, are helping these people back to normal, self-accepting lives. For most, just coming to a meeting and finding out that they are not the "only one"—sharing with someone, for perhaps the first time in their lives—is a healthy first step out of the closet and back to recovery through group acceptance. The social climate needs to change in order to allow more of these men and women to come forward.

"The warmth and understanding I have found from other birthmothers is, to me, incredible. For the first time in twenty-seven years I know there is nothing wrong with me for not 'putting it behind me and forgetting.' For the first time I can grieve and be understood, and

97

listen and understand, and NOT BE ALONE."—
A.D., Westchester, NY.

we meet
ordinary women who share one experience
we have all lost children
to the adoption system
each one has the same sorrow
in her eyes
sorrow the world denies expression
a longing
to know the lost baby
some of the children have grown up
some are found
some have been seen
I have a picture only
but arms are still empty
we share excitement
as a search succeeds
a mother draws close
to finding her child
once three
some have not begun
they have come
because here we can say it out loud—how it feels

we discuss our distances
(fifteen years, 3000 miles, nineteen years,
thirty-four years,
nineteen years, 2500 miles, eleven years, 1500 miles,
I don't
know ANYTHING)
we can't time travel
or replace that baby
the baby is grown now
but we can talk
and we can help each other
because we know that pain
and we are getting wiser
smarter
cagier
and we will find

those that look
and those that grieve still
can begin to share
their pain
that's why we meet

crystal 3/24/84[34]

THE SEARCH

"Much of my pain could have been eased if I had known she was alive, healthy and happy, if her adoptive parents had sent updates to the file at the Children's Bureau. Then I could have waited more patiently for her to contact me when she was ready. Because I still don't know anything about her except, finally, that she is alive, I need to see for myself that everything has worked out for her happiness."—Sandy Cox, Wilmington, DE.

"Experts are beginning to acknowledge what . . . birthparents have long known: the pain of surrendering a baby for adoption is neither forgotten nor diminished with time. Rather, it's grief that endures throughout life and often leads a woman on a frightening and often all-consuming search for the son or daughter she surrendered."—Kate Weinstein.[35]

While stimuli regarding search and reunion are coming at us all the time, one must be ready to accept the input. This often happens upon reaching a certain age or stage in life such as the thirties, which are said to be a time of introspection and tying up the loose ends of one's life. A search may also be triggered by a special event such as a death, birth, divorce or move.

Birthparents who become aware of a network of searching adoptees and birthparents may proceed quickly or they may take years to take even a first step. For many, the first step is joining a search and support group, while others may search on their own. Either way, a common avenue eventually takes most back to the attorney or agency who handled the surrender. This is necessary in order to get information pertaining to their children's welfare; to get "non-identifying information" about the adoptive couple, i.e., age, professions; and to submit a waiver of confidentiality. This document, which most agencies will agree to place in their files, allows the agencies to give the birthparents' names to their children should they return and request same. For most women, returning to the agency is unpleasant at least, and traumatic for some. Some women become physically ill upon returning.

Agencies, and workers within the same agency, will give varying degrees of support to "returning" birthparents and adoptees. Attorneys who handle independent adoptions are known to be less cooperative and often have no records or files available to a returning birthparent or adoptee.

When I became aware of a network of searching adoptees and attended some of their meetings I began to question that which I had numbly accepted. Could all of our children have been placed in loving Jewish homes or good Catholic families? I slowly and sadly began to recognize that these were the great white lies told to birthparents, just as many adoptive parents used to have a standard story they told their children about us: "Your mother died in childbirth and your father was killed in the war (or in a car crash)." Convenient little tales to end curiosity. Lies told with the best intentions. One birthmother, who searched on her own, discovered that her child's adoptive father, whom the agency had claimed was "in a helping profession" was in fact a police officer. Another, whom an agency called a diplomat, turned out to be a bartender!

"I have tried to deal with my agency. I have written letters that they haven't even answered. When I went back there to speak with them in person, after all these years, they treated me as if I was still seventeen. They insulted my intelligence by telling me bold-faced lies and insisting that I was the first one who ever returned to the agency asking information! They tried to make me feel abnormal for caring. I started to feel dehumanized again, so I left."A.W., Westfield, NJ.

Many agencies will accept a waiver of confidentiality from returning birthparents if the birthparent knows to request it. This is a notarized statement which, when placed in the agency file, alleviates the agency of their responsibility to protect the confidentiality or anonymity of the birthparent. Theoretically, if such waivers are on file when searching adoptees contact their agencies, the agencies violate no statute by releasing the information. Even without a waiver on file, the handling and disbursement of information contained in the so-called "sealed records" are agency policy and vary from one agency to another.

I myself began as a "passive searcher," taking comfort in believing that I had made myself available to my daughter should she need or want me because I had placed such a waiver on file with the agency handling my daughter's adoption placement. I was soon to come to another sad realization. In order to avail themselves of information left with the agency, adoptees need (1) to know that they are adopted, (2) they need to know which agency handled the adoption, and (3) they need the courage to overcome their fear of rejection in order to go to that agency, sometimes against the express wishes of their adoptive parents, or just sensing that it would hurt their parents. In addition to all of these obstacles, a waiver placed in the file is no guarantee that the agency will in fact reveal the desired information upon request.

"I had written to the agency several times, notifying them of my present address and my married name. I was very concerned when I discovered that I was diabetic and pleaded with them to notify my son's family. They said they would put my letter in his permanent file. When my son found me he was twenty-seven. He said that he had been to the agency when he turned twenty-one and asked for my name and they had told him I was a good swimmer and was tall."—J.W., Baytown, Texas.

Not every birthparent dares to search. Many do not know that they can; some believe they have no right to. Some believe that their children can easily find them, if they wanted to. (Ironically, many adoptees put off searching, believing that their mothers could easily find them!) Other birthparents and adoptees are paralyzed by the fear of rejection, while a small percentage of birthmothers (fifteen percent, according to Sorosky, Baran and Pannor) fear the loss of their anonymity. Those who search, state most often as their motivating factors a desire to ease their fears and concerns about the well-being of their children and to ease the curiosity of their children.

Death by Adoption, by Joss Shawyer, considered by many to be one of the most radical books on adoption, states in its introduction: "It became apparent that (birthparents) suffer deeply from what I now believe is an unresolvable grief. Unresolvable, that is, until they meet their children again." The belief that reunification would naturally be equated with birthparent healing is, however, sadly false in a great many instances.

The culmination of a search, while often satisfying for adoptees who search to find themselves, is not always so for birthparents. Birthparents who complete a search are often surprised to find that, rather than an ending for their grief, their grief is renewed all the more. Some wonder if there is something wrong with them. "I've finally found the son I've longed for for twenty-seven years and I'm more blue now than I was before,"—M.W. of Ridgefield, NJ. Why, she wondered? What's wrong?

What is "wrong" is that in finding a full grown offspring such mothers have to finally accept the loss of their babies. They have to grieve all of the tears which were locked inside them all those years. The realization of what they have lost stands before them. Gone forever are his diapers, his wobbly steps, his cooing, his scribbled drawings, his cut knees, braces, zits and dates. The loss of the parenting experience must be mourned.

Without search a birthmother can fantasize on her lost

child. But those who search and find, whether the reunion is reciprocal or not, are learning yet another kind of pain . . . they have lost not only their babies, but their adult children and their grandchildren as well. Is it any wonder that Rynearson has called the birthmother experience unresolvable grief? Unresolvable in many cases, even after reunion.

Birthparents also need to enter into their search, just as adoptees do, with the realization of the possibility of rejection. Although statistics again are lacking in this area, there seems to be a greater "success" rate when adoptees initiate the search rather than when the birthparent does. However, as Chapter Five indicates, concerned birthparents cannot always afford the luxury of waiting until they are found by their children. However, like adoptees, most birthparents agree that no matter how "bad" the end results are, knowing —even knowing the worst—is always better than not knowing. This is true of birthparents who have found abused children and of those who have found deceased children.

The end results of the birthparent experience are yet to be known. Birthparents may share some similarities with Holocaust survivors, with survivors of incest and rape. Atrocities such as these leave their mark not only on those who survive but also on their offspring. Gail Davenport believes that some of the subsequent, kept children of birthparents may, like other survivors' children, feel a great sense of guilt. "Why was I kept and he given away?" Still others, she fears, may live to replicate their parents' experiences. These are some of the many issues that need further study before surrender continues to be promoted as the "winning choice."[36] At the same time, there is a need for society to begin to listen to birthparents and to try to understand them. While birthparents see themselves as victims, they are often viewed by society as perpetrators.

4

Adoptive Parenting:
Overcoming the Obstacles

". . . Heredity or environment—which are you a product of?
Both, my darling, both
*   They're just different kinds of love. "*—Legacy, anon

I share the view of Mary Benet, when she says that ". . . adopters need not fear that a look at adoption as a political phenomenon will cast them as the villains of the piece . . . Adoptive parents do not have to shoulder the blame for family break-up and the relinquishment of children. Rather, they can help place the blame where it belongs: on a social system that impoverishes and punishes certain groups of people. Armed with the facts about adoption, they can help to change that system and to make adoption part of a more humane and realistic alternative for children and their families."

Adoptive parents, perhaps more so than any other parents, desire to do their best. They have become parents through diligence and long waits, sometimes involving great expense, sometimes enduring much emotional stress. None become parents quickly, easily, or by chance. There is little doubt that most try their best to carry out their responsibilities. But they need more help than they have gotten. Changes are occurring in agency procedures, particularly in the areas of sharing of information and in post-adoptive services, but often they are too few and/or too late.

Howard James, writing about child abuse, states that "few subjects of such importance are more neglected in America. We too often assume that parents—like robins and rabbits—will automatically do the right things for their offspring . . . Adoption may provide a child with permanency, a sense of being wanted, of belonging, but like foster parents, few adoptive parents are helped or trained."[1]

A 1981 issue of the newsletter of OURS, one of the nation's largest adoptive parents groups, deals in depth with a specific case of terminated adoption. The story is told by parents who had adopted three air-lifted Vietnamese children and then discovered that they were expecting their first biological child. One of the three adopted children, Susie, was adopted at the age of two after being in a foster home and an orphanage. She was malnourished and in poor physical and emotional condition when she reached her new family in a new country.

The article stressed the parents' feelings of being ill-prepared for the obvious problems of taking a child with so many handicaps, and of their strong belief that love could cure all. Susie is described by her parents as being jealous, vicious and naughty as exemplified by destroying plants in the home and urinating "inappropriately." They describe their attempts at spanking, lecturing and isolating the pre-school aged child to no avail. At this point, feeling hopeless and fearful for the safety of their unborn child, they consulted their social worker who asked if they had considered terminating the adoption. Susie was five years old when they terminated the adoption.

In this case, the parents recognized that a major factor of the adoption termination was their inadequate preparation and their unrealistic expectations. With the number of waiting parents far outweighing the number of available children, agencies need not fear "scaring off" potential adopters by being honest with them about the difficulties of parenting non-related children. On the contrary, they would be providing a well-needed screening process and helping to lower the rate of terminated adoptions.

There is also a need for restructuring the framework wherein adoption workers offer the alternative of termination to an adoptive couple. Certain circumstances are unique to the adoptive family and the first step in helping to overcome potential problems is to recognize these differences. For years, social workers perpetrated a cruel hoax on adoptive parents by telling them to "take this child home—it is the same as if it were born to you." Likewise, the public is told that adoption's main purpose is to provide permanency for the child. Yet, in these contentions lies another adoption irony. If the child is for all intents and purposes legally the same as if it were born to the adoptive parents, why is termination suggested as an alternative? I can think of no blood-related family experiencing the most severe acting-out on the part of a pre-schooler being given the suggestion by a professional to surrender their child to adoption as was suggested to Susie's parents.

Mary Walker, adoptive mother and founder of the Center for Adoptive Families, New York, finds that "the terms 'adoption disruption' and 'adoption failure' are derogatory and non-productive. We are trying new, positive ways to help families through a bad period."[2] The center holds conferences and offers workshops to help adoptive families whose children, adopted as infants, are now acting out as adolescents, and helps older children adjust to new families.

Tom Regan, Marjorie Mereen and Mary Abbett, Children's Home Society of Minnesota, find that "families who communicate well with their social worker and agency; i.e. the families who know how to use, complain, get attention for themselves from the professionals, parent support groups and others, have a very low rate of failure. The family that takes the child and disappears, a family not open to outside advice, has the higher rate of failure."[3]

Marge Moran and Connie Anderson, editors of OURS, believe that "perhaps the 'reality' of adoption—of parenting, of giving love—means the necessity of going into it fully prepared and aware of the possible risks." They recognize, however, that often it can be difficult to go back to one's adoption case worker and admit to problems. Many adoptive parents fear "they gave us the child; will they take her back again at the first sign of trouble—at the first sign we're not 'super parents!' But as clients, as 'consumers of service,' we have a right to demand and expect help from our agencies . . . ASK FOR IT! DEMAND IT!"[4]

Often the myths of adoption are so ingrained in adoption workers that, coupled with their eagerness to make a "match" and to bring joy and happiness, they forget that adoptive parenting is neither better nor worse than parenting children to whom one is biologically connected, but it is *different*. It is the differences which professionals need to prepare adoptive parents for and offer ongoing help to deal with. "Adoption is not identical with producing one's own child into one's own family," says John Triseliotos, author of *In Search of Origins*. "Not to recognize this reality is to romanticize adoption, and adoption literature abounds in such pretense."[5]

More resources such as that at the Center for Adoptive Families need to be made available to adoptive families. In the first year of its existence, the center counseled dozens of families during and after adoption. Sherry Bunin, president of the Center, has two sons who were born to her and two daughters who were adopted. "We are talking about a different kind of family," she said, "one in which the mother didn't carry the baby for nine months and that makes a hell of a difference, whether people want to face up to it or not."[6]

Dr. Herbert Wieder, a psychiatrist who has been studying the adoption triangle for over twenty years agrees: "The traditional blood-kin family is composed of one mother, one father, and their child or children. The adoptive family is composed of two mothers, two fathers and a child common to them. Although society, and to some extent adoptive parents, would like to pretend that it is exactly like a traditional family, it is the differences that are extremely significant in each member's life."[7]

Do adoptive parents have more difficulty dealing with emotional and physical problems than do biological parents? Perhaps. While all parents expect their children to grow into healthy adults, a couple who waits years for a healthy, white newborn, or who adopts one privately, expects just that: a healthy child, perfect. Prospective adopters are well aware that if they are willing to accept second best, "imperfect," non-white, older or handicapped children, they can adopt, and in most cases quicker and less expensively than the route they chose in order to obtain healthy, white infants. Expectations of perfection often leave adoptive parents ill-prepared to deal with unexpected problems when they arise.

In addition to expectations, another factor which contributes to failure is the prospective couples' reasons for adopting. Melissa Norvell and Rebecca F. Guy found that "initial motives for adoption are the most important determinants of successful adjustment."[8]

A prosperous, educated, intellectually vigorous adoptive father of two was married seven years without children: "Then slowly you find yourself worrying. What's wrong? Whose fault is it, mine or hers?" Then came the doctors, the tests, the failed attempts, the tension. Finally one doctor suggested adoption. His initial reaction was: *"Adopt? Us?* Take in somebody else's illegitimate kid and try to love it as though it were ours? The hell with it! . . . Then a whole new series of things begins to happen in your mind. You want a baby. If you can't have your own, you'll make one into your own. If he lives in your house, he'll be your own and you'll love it. Inside of a year we went to an agency and adopted."[9]

When couples adopt before coming to grips with their infertility, their children can become a constant reminder of what "could have been." When such a couple adopts, they place a heavy burden on the adopted child to replace the imaginary child, whose loss has never been properly mourned, rather than to be himself or herself. Ivan Sherick, PhD, found that "having adopted a child is likely to interfere with the gradual unfolding of the psychological state of parenthood. For adoptive parents there is, among other vicissitudes, the burden of having 'failed' as biological parents and attaching to 'someone else's' child."[10]

C.L. Englund, research consultant, found that "for the couple struggling with infertility the distinction between parentage and parenting becomes clear. Such couples are interested in both the process of parenting, in performing the role, as well as the production, having a biological extension of themselves. Only when they can set aside their concerns for having conceived the child themselves can adoption become a viable means through which they can assume the desired role of parents."[11] Some adopt to replace deceased children, or for the purpose of having children of a particular sex. Such reasons for adopting need to be screened as potentially dangerous.[12]

Often husband and wife do not share the desire to adopt to the same degree. One often "goes along" to please the other. There may be deep-seated and unresolved guilt, shame and blame resulting from the infertility, if procreation and genitivity is an important factor to one party in the marriage. Lois Gilman, author of *The Adoption Resource Book,* observes that "if you have been struggling to become pregnant, you've probably felt depressed, overwhelmed, guilty and cheated. There may be tension in your marriage. You may have harbored thoughts of divorce so that your spouse can find a more fertile partner." Resolve,[13] a national self-help group for people with infertility problems, recognizes that infertility encompasses feelings of sexuality, self-esteem, and self-image, as well as a desire to have children.

Adoption then adds to such an already tense household a non-related person. Add to that one small behavioral problem, a learning disability or hyperactivity (all common in adopted children) and it could spell disaster. The divorce rate of adoptive couples as compared to the general populace is an area of research that is totally lacking and needs to be investigated in order to make sound decisions about the future of adoption.

Children with particular temperaments who are being raised in their biological families, often, though not always, have parents who are able to recognize the same traits in themselves or in another relative. It is comforting to such parents and their children to be able to say and hear "You're just like your Uncle Joe." Biological parents have the added comfort of knowing that while Karen is as stubborn as her uncle, Joe did become a successful attorney! On the other hand, certain behaviors can be alarming to adoptive parents who do not know where such traits have come from or to what ends they can lead. Margaret McDonald Lawrence observed that for adoptive parents "their child is a stranger whose potential they cannot know but are free to fear . . . It is human nature to be suspicious of a stranger, and yet adoption practice makes the adopted child a stranger—to his parents, and to himself." Normal sexual interest on the part of a female adoptee can be viewed with great concern by adoptive parents who may believe that their daughter has inherited "bad blood."

Such problems are inherent in the sealed adoption system, not the adoptive parents. Adoptive parents cannot be blamed when they are victims of lack of adequate information. "It is not a universal truth," says Margaret McDonald Lawrence, "that adopting parents want a stand-in for a child who might have been. But because their own anxieties over missing blood ties have been reinforced by modern adoption practice, the majority of adoptive parents do choose to keep the curtain firmly drawn between past and present. They fear that their children would prefer their biological relatives and they do not want to take that risk. Those more courageous parents who have more confidence in the adoptive relationship would prefer to deal honestly with their children and recognize and value them for themselves. But they cannot choose to be exceptions. State laws have incorporated dishonesty into the regulations that govern adoptions."[14]

Adoptive parents need not blame themselves or think that they have "failed" when their children seek to know about their past. Instead, adopters need to learn to be prepared for and to accept their children's natural curiosity about their past as a healthy attitude, not as ingratitude or disloyalty.

The vast majority of adoptees under the age of twenty-five know that they are adopted, although there are always a few adoptive parents who wait for the "right moment" to tell their children and risk the inevitability of their finding out and feeling betrayed. Susan and Elton Klibanoff found that "adoptive parents find it much more difficult to talk about adoption than is generally recognized."[15]

There are differing views on the optimal time to broach the subject. Some feel that the language of adoption should be introduced during pre-school years in order to become familiar. Others suggest waiting until after five years of age because of concern that it could conflict with the Freudian "fantasy family" stage which generally occurs around that age. In any case, Triseliotis found that adoptees who were told prior to the age of ten had far less problems during puberty and adulthood than those who were not told until after that age.[16]

Margaret McDonald Lawrence recognizes the complexity of the situation for adoptive parents. "Separation anxiety is the legacy of the single honesty encouraged in adoption—the early telling of the child that he is adopted. The child's understanding of his marginalism and his insecurity in his relationship with his parents give rise to the emotional and behavioral problems of this age."

While many adoptive parents have no difficulty in telling

their children, some need help. I remember overhearing the conversation of a mother who had one adopted son, and one born to her. Her adopted son, age ten, had seen the after-school special "Mom is Having a Baby," and asked if he had come out of her body like that. "No, you didn't," she answered, and had to leave the room to hide her tears from him. "Did my brother?" he asked, following her. "Yes," she said, and nothing more.

Adopted children need to know that they were adopted, yet born too, rather than the message given in many children's books on adoption that there are two ways to form families: birth or adoption. Ivan Sherick, PhD, tells us "that the condition of being an adoptee is neither 'average' nor 'expectable' and yet the child who knows of his adoption must deal with this unnatural condition in order that feelings about the self and the emotional bond with the adoptive parents are not ruptured irreparably, with serious consequences for further healthy psychological development. At some level the adoptee must have conflicting representations of himself, namely, 'rejected' by his biological parents and 'chosen' by his adoptive parents."[17]

The chosen child theory, until recently, was thought by adoption professionals to provide the adopted child with self-esteem. Instead, it often makes adoptees feel as if they must live up to being as perfect as they were chosen to be, often creating a great many high achievers among adoptees. The implication that adoption placement is in the child's "best" interest, suggests that there is something "bad" about the adoptee's origins, and thus something bad about themselves. (The same impression can be given later on when adoptees are warned not to search because they might not like what they find.)

The most current literature on the subject, which warns against using the phrase "given up for adoption" when telling a child about his adoptive status, suggests instead that adoptive parents tell their children: "Your parents knew they could not care for a child properly, so they made an adoptive plan."[18] Perhaps as an adult, one might intelligently reason that there was caring involved in making such a decision.

Because children are more emotional than intellectual, many internalize the rejection. How much better to be able to say, "Your original mother loved you very much, and wanted you very much, but was too young (or whatever the known circumstances are) and was advised that it was best for you to have two parents who could give you the things she couldn't."

Dr. Povl W. Toussieng, a child psychiatrist at Menninger Clinic, found that adoptive mothers who compulsively repeat "I chose you" are driven by a feeling of generalized guilt and are trying to quiet their own feelings rather than their children's. What they really may be saying is "I rescued you—so please be grateful, for I need to be forgiven."[19]

No matter how children are told, difficulties often arise when they reach seven to ten years of age and begin to ask more questions about their origins. Adoptive parents who receive no counseling in the handling of these ongoing questions, and who react by ignoring the subject or showing displeasure, are risking grave psychological damage to the children entrusted to them. Many adoptive parents are prepared to tell their children once and get it over with, and are not prepared for their children's need to update information. Laura L. Valenti finds that "sooner or later, most children come around to the matter of the biological mother's relinquishment. How they perceive this is a central issue of the entire adoption information question. Several approaches have commonly been used in attempting to explain the biological mother's reasons for relinquishment. They seem to fall into three categories—the good, the bad, the impersonal."[20]

David Brodzinsky, a psychologist who has studied adopted children extensively at Rutgers University, concludes that when children are old enough to understand what adoption means they suffer a mourning period over the loss of their original family. Adoptive parents need to be made aware of this so as not to interpret it as disloyalty to them.

Joan Calder, M.S.W., Children's Aid and Adoption Society of New Jersey, finds that parents who can recognize and grieve for their own loss of fertility are better able to understand and support the adoptee in mourning.

Sex education is another area of difficulty for many adoptive parents.[21] Parents who have not come to grips with their own infertility may find particular pain in discussing the subject. For many adoptive parents, to verbalize the fact that their child grew inside another woman's uterus is difficult, if not impossible, and they get little or no help with this from social workers or doctors. Many, therefore, simply avoid the issue, thus denying their growing children what they need in order to feel a connectedness with humanity.

Children, however, receive messages from their parents, even if those messages are non-verbal. Adopted children who are left with silence, or who see that their questions are upsetting to their parents, quickly learn not to ask and from that point on close up a part of themselves to their parents and often to others, feeling perhaps like "strangers in a strange land." "The (adopted) child," says McDonald, "feels his loss as a profound loss and he knows that his parents have been party to it. The task of acquiring individual identity is handicapped by the knowledge that loved parents have placed no value on the unique identity and history to which he was born . . . How can parents possibly persuade a child that they love him for himself when they don't want to know who he is?" In extreme cases, this can lead to difficulty in forming lasting relationships.

Jean Paton thinks "of search as accompanying the process of sex education. It's a natural thing. When a child asks sex questions you begin to answer them and include something about his own procreated background, how babies come into the world, how he came into the world, and that there were some real people and what they did, and so forth. So, at various ages, to various degrees, you talk about other parents along with his own sexual development. If this is omitted, the adoptee has a distorted view of sexuality, a distorted view of procreation, and a distorted view of his responsibility as a parent."

"Young adopted children," she continues, "who know they have other parents, have this strange, crazy notion that they are responsible for the disappearance of the other two parents. They may even have thought they killed them. Often this notion is not corrected. These children don't talk to anybody about it . . . nobody talks about it . . . they bury it . . . During adolescence it has to be dealt with."[22]

Paulina F. Kernber, M.D., in an article entitled "Adoption: A Lifelong Process of Adaptation," writes: "Adoption is not a circumscribed event that begins when legal papers are signed. Adoption is a lifelong process of adaptation that may require professional help for the successful resolution of the adoptive child's two all-consuming questions: 'Who were my parents?' and 'Why did they give me away?' Depending upon the child's temperament, experience, development, and environment, the way these pivotal questions are answered affects learning, family relationships, and the child's own sense of identity and self-esteem . . . Basically, to the child, to be adopted means to be rejected, and parental reassurance may have no more than a temporary effect, for the child has intense doubts about acceptability."[23]

Brodzinsky researched children's cognitive understanding of adoption and found at least one little adopted girl who thought that *all* children were born to one set of parents and raised by another. One can see why great care must be taken in how adoption is explained to a youngster.

Susan and Elton Klibanoff summarize what most adoption professionals are now advising adoptive parents: "There is no reason for you to feel uneasy, embarrassed, uncomfortable, or defensive when your child begins to ask questions about his biological parents. There is nothing against you in his questions. He is not challenging your right to be his parents. He knows you are his real parents, his family. He is merely trying to find out about those who gave him life. He has the same curiosity about his biological parents as any of us may have about our grandparents and great-grandparents. The very fact that he is asking demonstrates a great deal of trust and confidence in you. When your child questions you about his origins, answer truthfully."[24]

Adoptive Parents for Open Records, Inc. (APFOR),[25] was formed by families who recognize that adopted persons must incorporate dual heritages of adoptive and birth families as indicated in the following statement by member Sue Wright. "Through adoption we, as adoptive parents, are empowered to nurture another's child. With that power comes a responsibility to acknowledge to our children that they have two families—the one they were born into and the one they are nurtured by." APFOR families know that adoptive families are strong through love, not blood; support open adoption and open records; and aid adoption-separated families in search and reunion.

The journal *Family Relations* reported in 1984 that the majority of adoptive parents felt "anxious and threatened" about proposals to allow adult adoptees access to their original families. Many adoptive parents I have met, however, are prepared to answer their children's questions when and if they arise. This sounds, on the surface, the sensible approach. However, adopted children often fear that asking will hurt their parents, and may wonder and fantasize without verbalizing their doubts and fears. A sensitive adoptive mother told me that she looked for an opening to broach the subject with her silent teenage son. One day, observing him staring at himself in the bathroom mirror, she said, "I bet you're wondering who you look like?" Some children will ask for what they want and need, others may need reassurance that it is a "safe" subject to discuss without offending and may need assistance. Waiting for children to ask may not always be a safe indicator of necessity.

Some adoptive parents are concerned that by giving too much information they risk "losing" their children to the birthparents, either physically or emotionally. They fear alienation of affections. They fear that in the end, they will have been merely glorified foster parents. There is also concern that the information could hurt their children.

Such fears are understandable yet unfounded. The adoptive parents are the true psychological parents. Children who are raised in open adoptions from the very beginning, accept the birthparent(s) as one accepts any extended family member, but it is the daily provider and comforter that fills a special role which none can replace. Khalil Gibran reminds us that our children, biological or adopted, are only on loan to us, we do not own them. Just as one mother can love many children, our children can love more than one set of parents. Knowing—even knowing the worst—is always better than not knowing anything at all. Susan and Elton Klibanoff sum up the current professional stance in regard to openness in adoption today. "The common feeling today is that knowledge of his biological origins is good for the adopted child when it is made a part of his upbringing."[26]

In order for adoptive parents to reduce adoption-related problems, they need to:

- Analyze their reason for adopting. Is it to parent a child or to replace a fantasy child?

- Analyze their feelings about infertility and recognize that adoption is not a cure.

- Get as much background information about the birthfamily of their children as possible in order to be prepared to answer inevitable questions. Meet the birthparents if possible.

- Remember that adoptive parenting is different than parenting biological children.

- Be open with their social worker and ask for help when needed.

- Be prepared to be open to continued discussions about adoption—not one "telling."

- Let their children know that they are open. Don't wait for the children to ask; some never will.

- Analyze their fear of losing their children to the birthparent(s) and their feelings of guilt for having taken them from them.

- Help their children to normalize and solve their curiosity.

- Share with their children any and all information about

118

their origins and help them to obtain the answers they need.

Adoptive parents, such as Carol Gustavson, founder of APFOR, acknowledge "the fact that our children were born into existing families before they were placed through adoption . . . We have been denied many important considerations living under the existing sealed records law. We could only come to recognize the shortcomings as we raised our children and personally lived with their needs that we were unable to fill or love away."

The following letter was written by Jerry R. Herman, Akron, Ohio.[27] Although addressed to his adoptive parents, this letter was never given to them, as protecting his adoptive parents was always a high priority. Jerry wrote this to help clarify his own thoughts and feelings and to promote communication and understanding between members of the triangle:

"Dear Mom and Dad,

"Hi! I'm your adopted son. Of course, you know that! You even told me a long time ago. You said, 'That couldn't hurt, me knowin' that.' Today I turned thirty-five; yesterday, I was thirty-one . . . Some time ago I found my birth name . . . found my birthmother. But today I found my sister. I know their names, where they live. Course, you knew these things. You almost told me once, twice . . . or maybe even a hundred times. Almost! But not quite! You said you didn't want me to get hurt, and that's okay. We both knew that you really didn't want me to hurt you, to betray you, be disloyal, ungrateful, unappreciative . . . unthankful! So you kept silent while I was wondering, searching, asking, hoping.

"I was four when I came to you. You told me that. Couldn't hurt! All my friends were 'zero' at birth; I was four at rebirth. I didn't exist until I was four. No Mom . . . no Dad . . . no sister . . . no dog . . . no cat . . . no wettin' the bed, no cartoons, no one-year birthday . . . no nothin'. The law says I'm a new creature because I was four and adopted. The law says 'we' are just as if we had always been from the start. You told me that. A bunch! That didn't hurt.

119

"Did you know that my Mom used to sell ice cream at the same place I go to sometimes, and did you know that my sister's Dad is a lawyer, and that her Mom is a musician, and did you know that my sister was a cheerleader for the high school football team? You know, the one who beat us 28-12 my senior year? Yeah, you knew. You almost told me once, or twice . . . or maybe even a hundred times. But you didn't want me to hurt you.

"I started hunting for my first mother when I was eighteen. I've thought of my sister every day since I was ten—since the day you told me I had one—back when I couldn't hurt you. I found my mother eight years ago. We've spent some time; we write and stuff . . . I think she's neat! She thinks you're great! She loves you for doing what she could not do when I was four. She has thought fondly of you for thirty-one years. Course, I never told you. I didn't want to hurt you.

"Today I found my sister. This afternoon. Only about an hour ago. Took a long time. I got tired a lot. Spent a lot of money. I think I even cried a couple of times when I thought I couldn't find her. Course, you could have phoned her for me—anytime! But I know about you not wanting to get hurt and all.

"Hey! Thanks for taking care of me, and being my Mom and Dad! I am grateful, and more. I am appreciative, and thankful. I did not want to betray you, or be disloyal to you. I do feel guilty . . . I'm not sure why, but you said I should. I do feel guilty. Course, I made you a little happy, too, didn't I? I mean, you always said I gave meaning to your life. Filled a void—an ache in your heart—a yearning for a child. All those trophies and awards, they do mean something, don't they? You always said you had been blessed. Parent talk, huh?

"My head banged a garage door once. 'Smack!' No pain, no blood. The load of ball bats I was carrying clattered spastically to the concrete before the impact became conscious reality . . . shock . . . momentary oblivion . . . a brief second of pure nothingness. That's how I felt today when I began telling you about my sister, and you juttingly interjected her name! You told me in a minute things it took me seventeen years to find. You said you knew, always knew. Knew clear back when I was eighteen going on fifteen. Before even then! I guess you never understood how important this was to me, how I longed to tell my birthmother that I was alright, that I could feel her frustration, her yearning, her desire for reassurance as she made a decision, signed some papers. Let go! I had to set her at rest. Had to! And my sister? Really! Nothing can destroy this sibling instinct! She was as innocent as I. She didn't sign a paper; made no statement 'we think it is better if . . .' She just went . . . as I went. She said she thought she was coming back. She is! I almost mentioned this once, or twice . . . or maybe a hundred times. But I didn't want to hurt you.

"Today my sister filled a haunting void with her first incredulous trembling words of recognition. A doctored birth certificate never made me feel it was okay to be born at age four. Have I hurt you? I'm sorry! I still love you; I'm just not sure what to believe from now on . . . Who hurt you? I didn't hurt you! I said 'what do you think my parents were like?' You said, 'search, and betray us' . . . I said, 'I need to fill a void with knowledge and understanding.' You said, 'and toss us away' . . . I said, 'I need to empathize, hold accountable, forgive, maybe even love!' You said, 'maybe this is a mistake'; maybe 'we' were a mistake.

"I did search. I have learned. I do understand. I empathize, forgive, hold accountable, and thank God, even love . . . You, too, I love, even more. I better understand the risk you took, the specialness you possess. Thank you! I did not hurt you! You hurt yourself! You didn't believe in me! I did not betray you! I am a person of great capacity! I can grow and learn and love on many fronts, simultaneously. I am not selfish with my feelings, with my empathy, with my loyalty. I did not toss you away! I merely filled a gaping wound—an identity void.

"As a child, innocent, my childhood was abruptly altered. A piece of me was sliced away. It vanished! As an adult, I replaced that slice . . . I tossed away nothing; I only healed myself! As a whole person, I can offer you more . . . You reject the piece I replaced. Can you but reject the whole also? I feel cheated. So much energy could have been put to good, success, people, learning. Rather, I feel like I have always been running on only three cylinders. It's my fault! I am responsible! But, part of me was always wondering, yearning, searching, fantasizing. Maybe, I'll tell you about it some day. Maybe we'll sit down and really get to know each other once, or twice . . . or maybe even a . . .

"Actually, I don't want to hurt you. Never did. Still don't. Maybe it'd be better if we just keep silent, maybe . . . You almost told me so much. If we have a good relationship could anything I might have found really have hurt it? If we have a bad relationship, then hiding the truth, restricting my efforts . . . keeping silent! How could that possibly have made the poor good, or even better? Damn, I feel lousy about all this!

"Yesterday I was only thirty-one . . . Today, for real, I am thirty-five. I found my first four years all by myself. Well, not really. Some people helped. But I did it! I feel like I can do anything now. Anything I want! Anything important! That's silly, isn't it? Course there are some things I can't do. I can't read your mind. And I can't understand your silence when I needed your support. Dear Mom and Dad, I still love you. I just don't understand why you never told me."

Because Jerry was adopted at age four there was a real piece of his life missing. Many of the emotions that Jerry expressed, however, and the family communication blocks which he describes are true of many adopted as infants as well.

Parenting adopted children adds one more challenge to a profession which has been recognized as one of life's most challenging. As with any such task, preparation helps one to be aware of and hopefully deal with situations when, or before, they occur. Laurie Wishard, adoptee, and her father, William Wishard, co-authors of *Adoption: The Grafted Tree,* suggest prospective adopters use the following self-evaluation questions as a guide to readiness:[28]

• Could I accept a child with interests and abilities very different from my own?

• Am I willing to accept outside help?

- Will I be able to talk to others and to my child about the adoption?

- For me, is adopting a child a first choice rather than second best?

- Can I deal with information about an adopted child's past?

- Does my husband or wife want to adopt a child (if applicable)?

  To their suggestions I add one more:

- Can I accept adoptive parenting as parenting a child with two sets of parents?

Part Three

The Families

"For love . . . is the blood of life, the power of reunion in the separated."—Paul Tillich

5

The Right
of First Refusal

"To see right and not do it is want of courage."—
Confucius

"All that the evil forces need to win the world is for good men to do nothing."—Edmund Burke

PAT AND PHIL[1]

Phil was born to Pat, a fifteen year old unmarried Floridian cheerleader from a good family who describes herself as having been a "goodie two shoes" and who became pregnant on her first sexual encounter with her boyfriend of four years.

Pat's parents gave her no choice other than adoption after she refused to have an abortion. Pat stayed at home, wearing ponchos to conceal her condition. When her "time came" she went to the hospital to deliver and after delivery was removed from obstetrics and placed in a room with a dying woman. Though she was not permitted to see her son, she snuck down the hall to do so but never got to hold him. When she refused to sign papers, the nurses called her parents.

127

Pat signed some papers while still in the hospital, and five days after giving birth she was taken to an attorney's office where she signed surrender papers. She believed that, because she was a minor, she was only releasing custody until she became of age, at which time she would regain custody.

When she turned seventeen, she approached her family and told them that now she was old enough to get her child back. They were shocked. When the realization hit Pat that it was forever, she tried to block it out of her mind. In 1976 Pat became phobic and an hysterical hypochondriac. Through intensive therapy she learned that all of her illnesses were because she believed that she would die never knowing her son.

In 1977 Pat married; in 1979 she gave birth to a daughter and in 1983 she bore another son. In August of 1983 the need to find her son became paramount. Pat announced to her parents and husband that she intended to search for her surrendered son.

Back in Florida on vacation she looked up the attorney in the phone book. He wrote her a two-page letter telling her that there were no records. She was determined to find her son. She knew nothing of search groups but was convinced that somewhere there had to be a record of his whereabouts and she would find him. She read *The Search for Anna Fisher,* and then read an article by Lorraine Dusky and began to call search groups and investigators all over the country. She eventually hooked up with *Searchline* in Texas, where she currently lives, and they helped her to locate her son.

Phillip, now fifteen, had been adopted by a preacher who divorced when Phil was six years old and was currently a juvenile counselor with Human Resources Services in Florida. Pat called the home on a pretext and spoke with her son. She learned that he was not very happy at home, flunking in school and generally a troubled child who knew that he was adopted. She called back five minutes later and told him who she was and they spoke for about an hour. The next day Phil's adoptive father phoned Pat. She anticipated the worst, but he said, "I just want you to know that you have really made our life complete." He told her that in August (the same month and year when Pat's need to search peaked) his new wife had gotten down on her hands and knees and prayed that Phil's birthmother would come into his life because he was such a disturbed child.

Later that same day, Pat spoke to Phil's adoptive mother who told her that Phil had ADD (Attention Deficit Disorder) combined with hyperactivity. Pat describes him as a slow learner with spurts of activity. His adoptive mother describes him as very, very disturbed and had him arrested once at age fourteen. His adoptive mother said he had a seventy-seven IQ, was a constant bed-wetter and she had him on heavy doses of tranquilizers.

Within one month, Pat went to visit. She describes seeing a very pitiful child. He was 5'4" with bright red hair and freckles. She took him home for a couple of days with her, her husband and her two other children. It was planned that he would spend the summer with her. He was an emotional mess and he had committed crimes. He did well with Pat but regressed when he returned home and was placed in a boy's home. Pat got in touch with the school counselors who had never seen Phil's adoptive mother. He was released into Pat's custody in June. His adoptive mother had given up all hope.

At home in Texas with Pat, Phil threw away his medication, and had only one incidence of bed-wetting all summer.

Phil returned home after the summer and made the honor roll the first semester in school. Then he started regressing again. It was planned that he would return to Pat the following June for summer vacation. In May his adoptive mother phoned Pat and said, "Come and get him and I don't want him back here, not even for a visit."

At age sixteen, Phil came to live with his birthmother. Pat put him into an alternative summer school to make up for the two years he had lost. He graduated on time. He bought himself a car and currently works for a major airline. Pat thinks he's just a normal teenager, not a scholar. Pat and Phil fight occasionally, but she says "that's because he's so much like me."

What would have happened to Phil had Pat not had the determination to find him?

JULIE AND JEFF[2]

Julie was sixteen years old and a high school junior when she became pregnant by her childhood sweetheart. They had been dating steadily for two years and had discussed getting married when she turned eighteen. Her untimely pregnancy suddenly changed all their plans.

Julie's family doctor made arrangements with Catholic Charities and Julie spent the last three months of her pregnancy in a maternity home. Friends and schoolmates were told that she was sick and no one, not even her best friend, knew the truth.

Julie told the social workers she would not surrender her baby but they told her that she was being selfish not to and she was offered no other alternatives. She always felt that it was wrong. She had loved her son's father and even if he no longer loved her, she still loved their child. "It is wrong," she said in an interview, "to give away a child that you love."

With tutoring, Julie graduated with the rest of her class and while no one knew, Julie could not forget. Four months after surrendering she met her husband. As soon as they were married, she decided to have a child and has two other sons. But she never forgot her firstborn son.

Approximately four or five years after surrendering, her need to know if he was all right became consuming and Julie returned to Catholic Charities for answers to the questions which plagued her. Was her son alive and being well cared for? She asked for the social worker who had handled her son's placement and was told that she was no longer with the agency. She tracked this woman down and asked her about her son. Julie was told that she should not concern herself because he had been placed with a wonderful family and that all the records had been destroyed by fire.

Julie went back to Catholic Charities and asked a priest there to act as an intermediary on her behalf. He told her that he would pray for her. Another agency director told her that the adoptive parents were Irish and Italian, that the agency had kept in touch with them for two years after her son's placement and that he thought they had another child.

The only "help" the agency offered was in the form of counseling sessions. After six months of being told that she was disturbed for not forgetting and putting it behind her, she quit going.

In the meantime she had become aware of many articles on adoption and began her personal education. Through a TV show, she learned that groups existed which helped reunite adoptees and birthparents. Through such groups, Julie located her son Jeff's family when he was twelve years old.

She drove past his home and found it disturbing. There was no sign of Jeff. She drove by again. Still the same eerieness about the house. Then again. Then one day on impulse, as she drove by the house, she stopped her car, got out and knocked at the door. Jeff's adoptive father answered. Julie asked for his wife, and he informed her that his wife had died when Jeff was four or five years old (just about the time when Julie felt consumed with concern) that he had remarried and that Jeff and his new wife did not get along.

Julie later learned that her son was told that he was adopted at approximately eight or ten years of age when, in an argument, his stepmother said to him and his sister, "I don't have to be nice to you. You're not his real kids anyhow!"

Julie was told repeatedly by Jeff's adoptive father and stepmother that he was a "problem child" and that, among other attempts at help, they had returned to Catholic Charities.

Because he was such a "problem," Jeff had been sent to military school at age nine. The following year the school closed. Having read about a boarding school in New Hampshire, they put Jeff on a bus for the school at age ten. During his stay at the school he contracted bronchial pneumonia and was bedridden with high fevers for six months. During Jeff's entire stay at the school his parents never phoned, wrote, visited, sent clothing or money, nor did they pay the tuition.

During Julie's first conversation with Jeff's parents, she was told that school was ending in one month and that they would have to pay to keep him there for the summer, so if

Julie wanted him, she could have him! But, they would not reveal to her the name of the school or the location until they were certain that she was serious about taking Jeff permanently.

Julie was apprehensive because of the grim picture his adoptive parents had drawn about Jeff, but she had no doubts about what she had to do. He was her son, the son she had always loved and never forgotten. She contacted an attorney the same day. Within a week she visited Jeff for the first time in twelve years and what she found was a polite, frightened little boy.

When school ended, Julie got temporary custody while she underwent a home study. After a nine-month uncontested waiting period, Julie adopted her firstborn son, who was now a member of her family, along with his two half brothers, who were delighted to have another brother. Jeff, now twenty, still lives at home with his birthfamily. He graduated high school on time and currently works full-time and attends community college. Julie describes him as a good kid who gets into normal trouble. She realizes now that the "problems" which were described to her were his adoptive parents' not his.

Shortly after settling into his new home, Jeff asked Julie to see if she could help the brother and sister he had left in his former home because he was concerned about their safety. His parents had adopted a girl named Kim two years after adopting him and then had a son of their own before the mother died.

Julie discovered that Jeff's adoptive father and stepmother were no strangers to the Division of Youth Family Services.

Kim had come to school in disarray and bruised often enough for the teachers to report it. As soon as it became evident that an investigation would ensue, the family voluntarily surrendered their adopted daughter, age ten, to DYFS. Soon after, the authorities were back at their house because they had locked their youngest son, aged eight or nine, in the basement and gone away for the weekend. Neighbors rescued the child from a bathroom window. The child was removed from the home by court order. His whereabouts are currently unknown.

Julie approached a caseworker who had been impressed with her reunion with Jeff and asked the worker to try to locate Kim's birthmother. The worker from DYFS said that Catholic Charities would not reveal that information. Julie resorted to the same diligence which had led her to find her son and within one week had located Kim's birthmother. Kim's birthmother was ecstatic to have been found and horrified at her daughter's situation. She immediately obtained an attorney to reclaim her child.

At this time, Kim had been through two foster homes and was in a third placement with a family who wanted to adopt her. Because of the many traumas in Kim's life, the possibility of finally having a loving home, and the fear of rejection again, Kim refused to meet her birthmother or even to have contact with her brother, Jeff.

Kim sadly felt unloved in her second adoptive home, believing they wanted her as a babysitter for their young children. She ran away several times and was eventually taken in by her boyfriend's family where she stayed until she married at eighteen. Two weeks before Kim's marriage, she contacted her birthmother. Her birthmother, and not her adoptive mother, was at Kim's wedding.

What would have happened to Jeff had Julie not defied agency policy to find him?

What could have happened to Kim had her birthmother been informed sooner?

A DEFECTIVE CHILD

In most states, the law provides that where an adopted child shows evidence of a mental deficiency or mental illness, resulting from a condition that existed before the child's adoption, the adoptive parents may ask the court to annul or set aside the adoption. One condition of this rule, however, is that the adoptive parents must not have known of the child's condition at the time of adoption. The usual way in which a judge determines whether the child's condition fits within the rule is by deciding whether the child's condition would make him or her "unadoptable" by an agency. The natural parents may have practiced fraud or made misrepresentations in connection with the child's medical history. If this is the case, then the court will be even more inclined to grant the adoptive parents' request to annul the adoption.[3]

It is interesting to note that adoptive parents can obtain children with a warranty and return policy while parents of birth receive no such guarantees and have to accept their children as they come to them. Also of interest is the assumption that if the child is "defective" the birthparents were intentionally fraudulent about the disclosure. Why assume that birthparents, who often do not see or hold their own children, would recognize retardation or mental illness in a newborn, when the doctors and other professionals who handle such placements did not?

CAROL[4]

Carol was twenty-three years old and single when she became pregnant for the first time. She was a registered nurse and had ample means of support. Because her child's father would not marry her, she decided to make restitution for what she had done and make something good out of something terrible by giving someone a child. To spare her younger brothers and sisters disgrace, she moved to another state with her aunt, got a job and investigated adoption.

Through a doctor, Carol was put in touch with an attorney who came and interviewed her when she was about six months pregnant. He assured Carol that she would be placing her child in a good home with Christian professionals who could support her child well. She never saw the lawyer again.

Immediately after delivery, while still under anesthesia, another lawyer appeared at Carol's bedside. This attorney told her that the original adoption had fallen through; that the people had changed their mind. This man, whom she had never seen before, told her that being under the effects of the

134

anesthesia would make it easier for her to sign the papers, that she would forget it easier.

According to doctor's orders, Carol never saw her son in the hospital. She attempted to go on with her life as she had been told. She met her husband, told him about her son and was married six months after her son's birth. She had three more children but every Christmas and on her son's birthday she had great feelings of sadness and guilt.

When he was about thirteen years of age Carol decided that her health problems warranted contacting her son's adoptive parents. She began to search. She applied for her son's birth certificate both from the state and the county where he was born. It was there under her maiden name! Normally, when an adoption is finalized, an amended birth certificate is issued listing the adoptive parents, and the original birth certificate is sealed. The fact that Carol's son's original certificate of birth was never amended or sealed was cause for concern that he could have died or never been adopted.

She went back to the lawyer who had handled the adoption and he said that he no longer did adoptions and he did not remember anything about her case. She asked if there had ever been a child who was placed for adoption who was not adopted. He said, yes, there had been one blind child who had been given back to the state. Carol then went to the county Department of Human Resources and asked them to search their records, particularly looking through state schools for the blind.

Later, Carol obtained the records from the hospital in which her son was born and they indicated that her child was born in good health.

Meanwhile a friend of a friend's lawyer offered to help. After months of searching he called and said that he had located her son and that he would transmit Carol's health history. He sent her a copy of what he had sent on. While this attorney intimated to Carol that her child was adopted and that it was the adoptive parents to whom he was forwarding the information, he never came out and said that. Carol thanked him and went no further because he had done this as a favor with no payment. In retrospect, Carol sees now that the real reason she accepted his vague answer and did not question was because she was terrified to find the truth.

Questions still plagued her. When her son was about sixteen or seventeen Carol underwent counseling in which she went through the whole grief process of surrendering her child. She attempted through therapy to "let go," to re-relinquish emotionally. But she still believed that when he turned eighteen he would possibly have a driver's license or something that would enable her to find him.

Just when she was about to give up hope, one of her leads led Carol to find her firstborn son in a state school where he had lived all of his life. He had been placed in an adoptive home, but the adoption was never finalized and he was made a ward of the state at three months of age when he was diagnosed as being profoundly retarded.

A friend of Carol, who also has a retarded child, intervened on Carol's behalf with the authorities at the school and Carol was permitted to visit her son. She currently stays at the school for extended visits and has brought her son home for Christmas. She is in the process of obtaining legal guardianship and hopes to move him to a school closer to home.

Despite all of the pain that Carol has suffered, she speaks kindly of the people at the state school who have cared for her son. They are not callous, she says.

With no anger she states that the people who made decisions about her and her son did not know her. She was willing and able to care for her son had she known the truth. She wanted adoption to be a "better life" for him and to make a couple happy. She did not want to "get rid of" an unwanted child. But no one cared enough for her or for him to find out. Carol's picture was in the newspaper announcing her marriage at the same time her son's adoption was being terminated. She was an employed registered nurse. She was very visible.

Through her agony, Carol sees the bright side. "I was so afraid of the unknown. The reality is not as fearful as the unknown. I've suffered a lot of pain but the phantom pain is gone. I feel like one whole complete person." Finding her son has brought her great joy. "He is just precious and I love him," Carol says. "He is my baby. He's sweet and he's cute. He's like a nine-month old baby, very loveable. He's pretty. And he's not suffering."

Carol did discover that it was an isolated chromosome which caused her son's retardation. While she is thankful that her three subsequent children are miraculously healthy, Carol is concerned that secrecy such as this in sealed adoption represents grave potential danger to birthparents' subsequent children. Because of her concern, she notified her son's birthfather who had just recently married. He now has the opportunity to receive genetic counseling.

Did Carol, her husband and subsequent children deserve to know the truth about her firstborn? Did he not deserve the love he was deprived of for nearly two decades?

GINGER AND SHERRY[5]

Ginger was seventeen when she surrendered her firstborn daughter to adoption. She wanted to keep her child but she was told by a social worker that as a minor she had no choice but to surrender. Ginger saw her daughter, Sherry, in the hospital and once when she was about six weeks old. She was a beautiful and healthy baby; the social worker and Ginger both agreed on that!

Within a year Ginger married. She called the same social worker and asked if she could get her daughter back if the adoption was not finalized. She was told that Sherry was in a good home.

Four years after surrendering, Ginger became pregnant again and called the same social worker, asking if there was any medical information from the first birth that would be of interest to her obstetrician about Sherry or the birth. She was told that she had a difficult delivery, but that there was nothing else to report.

Ginger gave birth to her son and before he was a year old he was diagnosed as mentally retarded. Because of this and because Ginger has a brother and a sister with mental retardation she was contemplating voluntary sterilization and needed more information to make this decision. She called the social worker and again asked if Sherry was a normal child. She was again reassured that her daughter was fine.

For the next seventeen years, Sherry remained in Ginger's thoughts. She imagined her in first grade. Each year Ginger celebrated birthdays with her daughter in her thoughts. Believing her daughter to be a senior in high school, Ginger began to search and soon after the Attorney General of Georgia called to meet with her about obtaining information on her daughter.

The reason the Attorney General was able to reveal information normally sealed was that the information was not sealed. It was not sealed because there was no adoption. There was no adoption because Sherry was severely retarded and was never placed for adoption. Sherry's condition was known to the social worker from the day she assured Ginger how beautiful and healthy Sherry was at six weeks of age.

At the time of Ginger's call one year after Sherry's birth, when Ginger was told that she could not have her child back because she was adopted, Sherry was in fact in a foster home and plans were being made to institutionalize her. When Ginger called four years after Sherry's birth and was assured again that she was fine, Sherry was still in foster care.

When Sherry was three, a public health nurse requested a conference with members of the agency, a psychologist and a representative from the mental rehabilitation clinic. The records state that the department of health "was concerned that this mother did not have other children. They felt she should be advised against this, yet this agency took the stand that we felt they should do this but use other background problems rather than this child because this would be breaking confidentiality this agency had promised the mother, and this was the way it was handled." Ginger comments, "If this weren't so serious it would be funny . . . If only they had been honest with me I would probably never have had another child and my son would have been spared the chronic suffering he has been through and faces throughout his life."

138

When Sherry was five years old she was placed in the same institution in which Ginger's mother's failing health had forced her to place Ginger's brother. For ten years Ginger went to the institution to visit and to bring her brother home for visits, never knowing that her own daughter was right there! According to the records, it was known that Sherry's uncle was a patient in another unit with the same condition. It was known that Sherry's "natural mother" visited her brother and there was concern raised that Ginger would recognize Sherry.

Ginger says, "Confidentiality cannot be used as an excuse for not telling me . . . I wanted Sherry and they knew it. Since she was not adopted, but in foster care, I feel I had a legal right to her . . . It didn't have to be that way."

Ginger was unable as of 1982 to bring Sherry home, much as she wanted to, because of her situation with her son, but hoped that this would change with time.

There are, I am sure, men and women who surrender children to adoption because they do not want to parent. Some children are involuntarily removed from abusive or neglectful parents. This does not mean, however, that all birthparents lack concern any more than the fact that a percentage of *all* parents are abusive and neglectful means that all are.

Julie, Ginger, Pat and Carol are but a small sampling of women who lost their children to adoption through no lack of love and concern for their children's well-being, but rather because of it. While they were not lacking in love, what they did lack was maturity, a situation that is almost always rectified with time. In time, they became mature, married and able to provide just as stable—if not a more stable—home than their children had otherwise been provided. Like the majority of birthparents they were each married within a year or two of surrendering, yet their need to know how their children were faring and their children's need for them were ignored. Why?

Because birthparents are often offered adoption as a "solution"; a permanent solution for temporary problems. Because society stereotypes birthparents as immature, unmarried and foolish and sees adoptive parents as mature, married and stable. While this may be true at one point in time, what is wrong with this perception is its stagnation. People do not remain frozen in time. They grow and they change. Few birthparents remain forever single and immature, while not all adoptive parents remain married and stable. Adoption plans must have a flexibility factor to allow for such change. They must have a Right of First Refusal clause.

Julie, Ginger, Pat and Carol are representative of many birthparents who surrender for one main reason: to provide their children with a *better* home than they are able to at the time. Like the majority of birthparents, they were willing and able to care for their children when their children needed them. Yet they were ignored. In Ginger's case it is clear that the authorities knew well of her continued interest, concern and marital status, yet it was deemed not in her best interest to know the truth.

Reinvolvement of the birthparent(s) can offer the potential of providing a stable home for an otherwise unwanted child. Isn't this the goal of child-care agencies? If the birthparent(s) were not capable or desirous of providing for a child whose adoption had failed, perhaps another member of the extended birthfamily would be. Birthfamilies should be seen as a resource, if for no other reason than to save taxpayers unnecessary expenditures by warehousing children who are no longer considered prime marketable commodities for adoption.

Ginger and Carol's cases point up the little-recognized need for medical information to be passed in both directions. It is widely recognized that a major reason to unseal adoption records is to provide adoptees with their medical history, but it is seldom recognized that birthparents are also denied medical information that could be life-threatening to their subsequent children. A surrendered child's death due to SIDS or Tay Sachs, or a surrendered child having any genetic

140

disease or disorder, is of vital importance to both birth-parents genetically, if not emotionally and morally. Parents not knowing that their first child died of SIDS would not know to monitor a second, thus jeopardizing, if not losing, the lives of their subsequent children. Parents who are unaware of a genetic disorder might not be tested for it, and thus, like Ginger, might unwittingly bring other defective children into the world.

A few birthparents, such as Julie and Pat, were lucky enough to intervene in time to save their children from lives in foster homes, institutions or boarding schools. Yet these women were cautious in speaking with me to reveal the final break in their search which led them to find their children. What ethics dictate that secrecy is more important than saving a child; that loving mothers need to be concerned that in order to save their children they are violating a policy or statute which was intended to "protect" their children? Many, such as Carol, were less fortunate. They were too late.

Jerry Sherwood is one such birthmother. Like Ginger, she was seventeen and unmarried when she gave birth and reluctantly surrendered her firstborn son, Dennis, in Minnesota. Like many birthparents, she said, "I always thought I'd see him again."[6] This was not to be the case for Jerry. Jerry's search for her son led her to the discovery that he had died at the age of two. But her investigation did not end there. A mother of four children, she was troubled by her first son's untimely death, which had been called "questionable" but which had led, at the time, to no further investigation.

Jerry persuaded authorities to re-open the case and Dennis' adoptive mother, Lois Jurgens, was charged and found guilty of murder by abuse. Jerry Sherwood's continued concern for her surrendered son and reinvolvement in the events of his brief life saw to it that justice was served in convicting his adoptive mother of murder twenty-two years after the fact. If a mother had not cared enough to unravel the truth a murderer would continue to walk free.

The Right of First Refusal would mean that any parent

surrendering a child for adoption would be notified if the adoption was not finalized for any reason; if the child died; or if the adoption was terminated for any reason, and they and their families would be considered as a first choice before any other adoptive home, foster home or institution was considered. This would give birthparents peace of mind and might therefore reduce the number of searching birthparents. It would also greatly help birthparents in planning subsequent children. Giving surrendering parents the Right of First Refusal endangers no one, hurts no one (physically or emotionally) and infringes upon no one's confidentiality or anonymity. It in no way lessens the role of total parentage of the adoptive parents because it would only reinvolve the birthparent if the adoptions were terminated.

Women who voluntarily surrender, and their children, deserve the Right of First Refusal. No child should be institutionalized or in foster care because it is assumed that if he was surrendered he was unwanted then or now.

Part Four

The Future

"The probability that we may fail in the struggle ought not deter us from support of a cause we believe to be just."—Abraham Lincoln

6

Adoption:
A Circle of Love

"I know. But I do not approve. And I am not resigned."—Edna St. Vincent Millay

"Some of us are more effective than others of us . . . None of us are more effective than all *of us!"*—Anon

Adoption laws were created with the welfare of children in mind. They were short-sighted, however, in failing to envision the growing needs of these human beings as they moved into adulthood. These laws now serve to enslave rather than protect these same children, grown into adults. Modern adoption statutes were created at a time when the mores of our culture judged heavily against illegitimacy and single parenthood. Just as the times have changed, so must the laws reflect those changes.

To recognize that some adoptions have failed, is to ask why, so as to prevent it happening again; it is not to say that the majority of adoptive parents are not fine, fit parents. To recognize that many adopted persons are dealing with feelings of rejection is not to say that the majority are not happy, well-adjusted people.

Margaret McDonald Lawrence, speaking at the American Adoption Congress, Washington, D.C., panel on Physical and Emotional Needs in Adoption, May 5, 1979, noted: "Teachers, physicians, families and neighbors—the people who come into close contact with children—have always believed there to be a higher incidence of emotional/ behavioral disturbances among adopted children than among non-adopted. To the first published evidence of this phenomenon in the professional journals of psychiatry and psychology, child welfare people responded with denial or with theories of causes arising from pre-natal influences or faulty adoptive parenting. The idea that the cause might lie in their own design of adoption was unthinkable.

"If the wrongs of adoption are to be corrected, they must be recognized by those professionals whose primary concern is the welfare of the children . . ."

In order to accomplish this, we must first compassionately uncover the realities that exist. We must put aside our opinions and personal prejudices for the sake of the children, the innocent third parties caught in the middle. It is imperative for all parties in the adoption triangle to try to understand one another and work together, recognizing that all of the parties to adoption are victims of the system, not adversaries.[1] When I speak of casting light on, or humanizing adoption, I speak not against any individuals or groups of people, but rather of an antiquated system which needs revisions, and in some cases society's attitudes which need to be altered.

Each of the problems set forth in this book has a humane solution. If the solutions which follow had been set down out of the context of this book, they would indeed seem radical. In view of the existing problems illustrated within this book, however, we must stop glorifying adoption and recognize it for what it is: a second-best solution for all. Given the option, most adoptees, adoptive parents and birthparents would not choose to have adoption as part of their lives. Although those already involved have had to make the best of it, most birthmothers would have preferred to raise the children they bore; most infertile couples would prefer to have been able to conceive and give birth to their children;

146

and most adopted persons would prefer to have been blood-related to those who raise them.

Adoption is currently being promoted as a solution for infertility and for unplanned pregnancy. Just as divorce cannot be offered as a cure-all for every marital problem, new societal solutions need to be sought for single pregnant women and infertile couples. Because every adoption begins with a tragedy, like divorce it should be a last resort to be used only after all preventative attempts to keep the family together have failed. Adoption takes children from one less than ideal situation (single parentage) and places them in another (non-related parentage). The best adoptions under the present system of secrecy and sealed records, are shrouded in fear, rejection, and pain for many of those involved. Margaret Mead said: "Even good social institutions are open to criticism, and adoption as we have institutionalized it is no exception."[2]

ADOPTION needs to return to its original goal of serving the needs of the children. The purpose needs to be to find homes for children who need homes, not to find babies for the childless. All efforts need to be made to find homes for the 36,000 homeless children in this country who are free for adoption. In order to achieve this, legislation needs to be passed to encourage and subsidize the adoption of "special needs" children, particularly in terms of medical expenses and insurance coverage for children with pre-existing medical conditions entering an adoptive family.

Because adoption remains a necessary institution; because it is complicated by emotions, and conflicting interests; and because it involves the welfare of innocent children it requires many safeguards. All adoptions therefore need to be handled through reputable and licensed state and religious agencies.

Jeff Rosenberg, adoption services director for the National Committee of Adoption states: "The Steinberg case (see Chapter Two) is an extreme example but it points to what can happen in any potential independent adoption. It points out the need for some real changes in our adoption system. Nobody should be able to take custody of a child before being professionally evaluated."

The current practice of private, independent adoption often employs the use of gimmicks such as newspaper advertising which act to lure women by offering financial remuneration under the guise of payment of services or loss of time. Police allege that Richard Gettlemen operated as a baby broker using newspaper classified ads to entice unmarried mothers to travel to Louisiana to surrender their babies which he later sold for $10,000 to $30,000.

In the *Morris County Daily Record* (New Jersey) the following ad appeared: "ADOPTION: Loving parent seeks to adopt white newborn girl to three years. Tony 999-9999." Because of the potential for pedophiles and other abusers to obtain children through such advertising, Senator Mary Goodhue, New York, is considering the introduction of legislation which will either ban the newspaper ads altogether or require that those who place the ads are pre-screened.

Other forms of independent adoption apply pressure by suggesting that large sums of money need to be reimbursed for medical expenses if the mother changes her mind and decides to keep her baby. Adoption laws, which now vary greatly from state to state, need to be standardized and regulated.

While maintaining high standards, licensed agencies can and should "borrow" those practices which currently make private adoptions more appealing, such as openness between adoptive and birthparents. Licensed agencies would arrange the placement only after both the adopting and surrendering parents had received family counseling from an objective and recognized source other than the agency making the placement, and the placing agency would then be responsible to provide on-going post-adoption exchange of information.

Waiting lists are long for the small trickle of healthy, white newborns available for adoption, and screening methods which are stringent may at times appear to be unfair when they arbitrarily discriminate by age, etc. However, rather than help infertile couples seek alternatives to waiting and screening, they need to be helped to realize that the well-being of the children is the foremost concern and that each child deserves only the best set of parents available. We need not fear that bringing the problems inherent in adoption to light will "scare off" prospective adopters. With fifty to one hundred couples vying for each available baby, only those who are willing to face the difficulties need apply.

FOREIGN ADOPTIONS need to be halted at least until homes are found for "our own." Our government sanctions prejudice and discrimination by perpetuating the myth that Asian and South American children are somehow "better" than Mexican American, Puerto Rican, Black or mixed-race children. At best, foreign placements are cultural genocide, generally severing children permanently from their roots. Americans like to pretend that foreign adoptions are saving poverty stricken children from starvation and/or life in the streets. If this were true, and our motives were truly altruistic, every effort would be made to save both the mothers and the children. If this were true, we would not see reports of atrocities such as that committed by lawyer Carlos Cesario Pereira who was arrested for black marketeering Brazilian babies. Cesario handled one hundred and fifty adoptions at an average price of $5,000 a child. Police claim that about sixty people worked for him, including women who "masqueraded as social workers to persuade poor women to give up their babies . . . Brazil has an abundance of abandoned children, including an estimated 300,000 who live in the streets. Most, however, are dark-skinned, and foreign couples generally prefer fairer babies. As a result, light-skinned infants are at a premium for would-be adoptive parents and unscrupulous operators alike."[3]

INFERTILITY needs to be recognized and dealt with as a medical problem similar to a disability, not a social problem. Fertility has been falling in most of the Western world for more than a century. Research needs to be done into preventative programs such as cleaning up the environment and finding immunization and/or cures for the newer and

149

more resilient strains of venereal diseases which are responsible in good part for the rising infertility rates.

There are at least two dozen Sexually Transmitted Diseases (STDs) that affect thirty million Americans. Untreated, these diseases are a primary cause of the infertility suffered by 4.5 million American women. Since 1965, the infertility rate among women twenty to twenty-four years old (the group that delivers a third of U.S. babies) has tripled. Chlamydia, which has been called the VD of the '80s, is the most common and the most dangerous STD in the United States today.[4]

According to a report in *People,* 15 April, 1985, chlamydia is spreading faster than AIDS or genital herpes. It is the leading cause of increasing numbers—triple since 1967 —of ectopic pregnancies in this country. It will affect three to twenty million Americans in 1986. As many as 150,000 women will become infertile as a result. It is estimated that five percent of all female college students have it. Symptoms often go unnoticed while fallopian tubes get destroyed. Half of all women made sterile by the effects had symptoms so mild that no one suspected a problem.[5]

Dr. Attila Toth, director of MacLeod Laboratory for Infertility at New York Hospital, concurs. "Untreated bacterial infections may be responsible for low sperm motility in up to thirty percent of infertile men. They can also kill sperm. Sexually transmitted chlamydia, mycoplasma or gonorrhea organisms are among the most dangerous."

It is estimated that fifteen percent, or one in every six couples of childbearing age, has an infertility problem. However, this figure seems to be based on the fact that a couple trying unsuccessfully to conceive for one year is considered to be infertile. Yet, Dr. William Andrews, Past President of the American Fertility Society, states that of one hundred couples, about eighty percent can get pregnant within a year. Another ten percent can get pregnant by trying for another year. The remaining ten percent have a fertility problem, half of which can be successfully treated in an uncomplicated way. The remaining half need more sophisticated treatment and, of these, about half will be able to conceive and half

150

won't. Thus, 97.5% of all couples seeking to get pregnant willing to go the last mile to conceive can conceive.[6]

Willard Cates, Jr., M.D., of the Centers for Disease Control in Atlanta, is among many who recognize that age is another primary factor in infertility, and often discourages couples from allowing the time needed to conceive. The number of American women having their first child between the ages of thirty and thirty-four has quadrupled over the last twenty years. Gynecologists and other professionals need to counsel sexually active women and couples who are opting to delay childbearing of the risk of future infertility they are facing from veneral disease; birth control methods such as the I.U.D. and the pill; and age.

Psychological counseling and self-help groups for the infertile need to view the loss of fertility as a loss to be mourned and grieved, perhaps forever. There is a need to separate the loss of procreation and generativity from the loss of the parenting experience. Only the loss of parenting can be replaced by adoption; all other aspects of childbearing are gone forever (except for those who are candidates for medical procedures such as in-vitro fertilization.) For those whose infertility problems cannot be helped by medicine, their loss of ability to reproduce may be final, and measures should be taken through therapy to reach resolution of that loss. Only those who accept adoption as an opportunity to parent, should be considered as prospective adopters. When one loses a limb or an organ, one can wait and pray for a transplant. But that limb or organ is transplanted from a donor who has died. It is unhealthy to expect the infertile to wait like vultures for a healthy white mother to relinquish her child to fill their needs. It is equally unfair to expect substitute children to be in every way the same as the originals which are lost and can never be replaced.

Preventing infertility needs to be prioritized, because in addition to its effects on adoption, the *New York Times,* 5 April, 1987, reports that "Federal officials say the rising demand (for babies) has also led to a proliferation of organized rings that smuggle babies, some of them kidnapped, across the Mexican border and then sell them to the highest bidder in this country."[7] The article further states that "according to adoption specialists, the widening gap between supply and demand has spurred not only the smuggling of growing numbers of babies from Mexico and other Latin countries but also the creation of a new kind of entrepreneur who helps couples find a baby, usually for a large fee." Some have murdered mothers both here and abroad (as documented in the film, *The Official Story*) to obtain their babies. The time has come to stop the exploitation of couples desperate for children, and to offer some real hope for the future.

REPRODUCTIVE TECHNOLOGIES are a result of medical entrepreneurs preying on the vulnerability of infertile couples, and seeing infertility as a vast new market. Reproductive technologies offer the promise that every couple, fertile or not, has a chance to have a child who is biologically connected to at least one of them, and many willingly undergo physical and financial hardships to obtain such a child.

It is curious that many people who are obsessed with the idea that their children be biologically linked to one of them, are very willing, at the same time, to ignore the other half of their children's ancestry. In making the later overturned court decision in the Baby M case of 1987, Judge Harvey Sorkow was impressed with the Sterns' ability to "protect" the child from ever knowing the sordid truth of her reality. How many children will be produced who will never know the true origins of their egg or sperm? A clinic in New York State which performs voluntary sterilizations is offering payment for the removal of eggs at the same time. Eggs and sperm must not be bought, sold or donated as one might do with blood, for eggs and sperm, unlike other bodily fluids, can create new human beings.

If adoptive parents enter into parenting with false expectations, one can only wonder about the expectations of parents who mortgage their homes and devote years of time and effort into creating offspring, rather than choosing to parent existing children. They obviously expect "their own" to be "better." In the Baby M trial, the child's father,

William Stern, testified to the importance of having a child who was biologically connected to him. He spoke too, of his hopes and plans for Melissa, the daughter he paid in excess of $20,000 to have carried by a surrogate mother for him and his wife. William Stern and his wife Elizabeth spoke of private schools, piano lessons and college. One can only wonder how they will feel towards their creation, Melissa, if her interests lie outside the adademic world. One can only speculate how the Melissa Sterns of the world will feel about themselves, how the "surrogate" or contract mothers will feel about themselves, how the "surrogates' " other children will feel and how all other adopted persons feel when such importance is placed on genetic connectedness.

Gena Corea, author of *The Mother Machine,*[8] has investigated birth and reproductive technologies extensively. She concludes, based on interviews with scientists and practitioners, that infertility is "the wedge." The inventors of invitro transplant, for instance, do not see the future market for such technologies limited to infertile couples. They see instead a way for couples, fertile or not, to choose the sex, educational level, and other physical characteristics of their offspring, creating "designer" babies. There looms before us the very real probability of genetic engineering. There likewise looms before us orphan asylums overflowing with unwanted and "undesirable" children.

While surrogate parenting and invitro transplants are relatively new, artificial insemination by donor (A.I.D.) has been practiced long enough for us to have the hindsight of knowing the feelings of those thus produced. While we will never know of the damage done to those who are not told the truth of their origins, we do know that some people who are aware that they were products of A.I.D. feel very much akin to adoptees. Some, in fact, have contacted adoption search organizations in a desperate, though probably futile, attempt at locating the men who donated sperm on a particular day in a particular city. The idea that they will be successful is absurd, but their need to know who their fathers are is as real as your need or mine to know who our fathers are. Many are driven by a need for medical history for themselves and/or for their children. There is also need for concern about incest among offspring as a result of numerous egg or sperm donations by the same individual.

Ethicist Robert Cassidy of the University of Medicine and Dentistry of New Jersey Robert Wood Johnson Medical School, said regarding surrogacy, "It is a shame if people can't have children. That doesn't mean that anything that will give them children is therefore right."

PREVENTION of many "unplanned" pregnancies could be aided through sex education programs and by the availability of birth control. However, the administration has proposed cutting federal family planning programs every year Reagan has been in office.[9]

The United States has the highest teen pregnancy rate of all developed nations—ninety-six per thousand in the nineteen to twenty-five age group. A study conducted by the Alan Guttmacher Institute and researchers from Princeton University's Office of Population Research, revealed that American teenagers are exposed to media messages that sex is "romantic, exciting, titillating" while at the same time "almost nothing they see or hear about sex informs them about contraception or the importance of avoiding pregnancy."[10] The study points out that those countries with "the most easily accessible contraceptive services for teenagers and the most effective . . . programs for sex education have the lowest rates of teenage pregnancy, abortion and childbearing."

Here in the states, The Adolescent Family Life Act (AFLA) was proposed in 1981 to address the problems of teenage pregnancy decided to "promote self-discipline and other prudent approaches to the problem of adolescent premarital sexual relations . . . (and to) promote adoption as an alternative for adolescent parents." This, despite the fact that even highly motivated couples using combinations of the more sophisticated natural family planning methods experience a pregnancy rate of fourteen percent. The AFLA prohibits the distribution of funds to groups that provide any abortion-related services, including counseling and referral,

154

or that subcontract with any agency that provides such services.

Patricia Donovan, Contributing Editor for *Law and Public Policy of Family Planning Perspectives,* wrote: "By funding only those organizations that promote adoption for pregnant teenagers and teenage parents, the law essentially makes a judgment that no teenage mothers are capable of successfully rearing their children and should, therefore, relinquish their babies to older, more stable couples. Certainly, it is well documented that teenage childbearing results in disadvantages for mother and baby. It is questionable public policy, however, to assume that all teenagers are unsuitable parents . . . By requiring grantees to encourage teenagers to choose adoption, and at the same time prohibiting them from discussing abortion or even making a referral for abortion counseling, the law denies teenagers information about the full range of options regarding their pregnancy."

In February 1986, the House Select Committee on Children, Youth and Families released a report on teen pregnancies which found that the pregnancy rate among fifteen to nineteen year olds increased from 99 per thousand in 1974 to 109 per thousand in 1979 and 112 per thousand for 1982. Yet they found that the nation has failed to devise a focused effort to stem the rising tide of teenage pregnancies, over half of which are to unmarried mothers. The committee's survey of state governments found that "prevention programs, including family life education, health education, contraceptive information and services . . . receive much less emphasis than programs for already pregnant and parenting teens." Chairman George Miller (D-CA) said more attention should be paid to preventing teenage girls from becoming pregnant. "We're spending billions of dollars but we're spending money to pick up the pieces. It's all to deal with the results of a tragic situation." Miller also said that school-based health clinics such as those in St. Paul, MN, and Baltimore have reduced school pregnancy rates by providing contraception and sex education.

Diane S. Burden, PhD, Assistant Professor of Social Policy and Research, School of Social Work, Boston University, and Lorraine V. Kellerman, Dr. PH, Professor of Public Health, Florence Heller Graduate School for Advanced Studies in Social Welfare, Brandeis University, found alternatives. For one thing they state that "access to family planning without parental consent appears to be an important factor in reducing fertility rates." Further, "If the poverty of female single parents and their children is to be alleviated, teenage mothers and their families must receive the financial and emotional support that will enable young mothers to complete their education, obtain job training and experience and avoid the pitfalls of early marriage and subsequent divorce. Policies that both increase AFDC (Aid to Families with Dependent Children) support and enable women to attain greater financial security gradually through employment and deferred marriage are required if the current slide of women and children into poverty is to be halted."[11]

Lenny Cottin Pogrebin, a founding editor of *Ms.* expresses her concern more cynically. She quotes Reverend Dan C. Ford of the Moral Majority as having said that he doesn't want women free to "kill the babies and to cover up the sin of fornication." To this she replies "That sanctimonious, moralistic declaration explains the national tragedy of one million children every year. To expose female sin, contraception is denied and abortion rights threatened. Unmarried girls' babies can be given up for adoption to a 'real' family. But first, the babies must be born to prove the girls have been bad."[12]

Others, perhaps more cynical still, have suggested that the current administration, headed by Ronald Reagan, an adoptive father, denies birth control and promotes adoption in order to supply babies for themselves and their constituents. Whatever the reason, we seem to be closing the barn door after the horse is out.

Dr. Wayne Decker, director of the Fertility Research Foundation cautions: "One important reason for infertility among women today is the idea that they can wait until thirty-five before starting a family. The fact is that a woman reaches her peak of fertility when she's twenty-four years old." Puberty begins up to three years earlier than it did at the time of the American Revolution. In view of this, and the fact that sexual desire also peaks during late adolescence and early twenties, would it not make more sense to encourage women to have their families during this time of peak fertility and delay their careers until their mid-thirties to forties when their children would be grown, rather than thwarting nature as we are now doing by attempting to arrange our lives the other way around?

Of major concern in teen pregnancies are the low birth weight, premature, and handicapped babies born to young mothers lacking adequate nutrition. Adoption of such babies will do nothing to improve this. Teenagers can and do make excellent parents if given the proper support. In other, less industrialized nations, women bear children when they are most fertile and healthy—in their late teens and early twenties. Anthropologist Dana Raphael has studied child-birth and childbearing in primitive cultures for many years.[13] Raphael found strong support systems among such people. The mother-to-be is generally surrounded by elder women of the tribe who pass on all their knowledge. At the birth, it is the women of the tribe who generally attend the birthing mother, not her man. Afterwards, during the first weeks or months of the baby's tender life, the women, or in some cases one woman, tend the new mother. The name of the woman who fills this very special role is the "Doula": one who mothers the mother. Perhaps we need some Doulas in our society.

Encouraging teen childbearing might seem a radical suggestion, but if our present social system continues to prevail, imagine what the future might hold. Young, sexually active women would be encouraged to surrender their children to older, more stable couples, deferring parenting until they were too old to bear children, or had become infertile from years of using birth control devices or having contracted one of the many sexually transmitted diseases, and then taking someone else's child. Thus, we could create a society in which no children would be biologically related to their parents. Or, with continued sophistication, we could freeze our sperm and eggs and sterilize everyone who reached puberty. Then, when we felt we had reached the point in our careers when we could financially afford to add children to our families, we would purchase eggs and some sperm—of the highest caliber of intelligence and good looks, of course—have them fertilized and incubated for us, and then, when they were not in day-care, perhaps enjoy their company on alternate weekends and be able to say with pride, "That's *my* kid!"

PRO-LIFERS need to see the value of life not just for the unborn, but for the mother as well. For, as one birthmother put it, "adoption aborts the mother instead of the baby." Offering today's single expectant mothers the choice between adoption or abortion is offering them a choice between the devil and the deep blue sea. The guilt, shame and recurring anniversary depression which have been documented to occur after abortion, are paralleled by those who lose children to adoption. While birthparents have not taken a life, they have broken a sacred bond between mother and child and often feel as if they have signed a death sentence with a pen. Death griefwork can reach resolution in time, but a limbo loss exists for mothers who do not know if the children they bore are dead or alive; happy, healthy and well, or not. Birthmothers are seldom at peace.

To be truly pro-life is to take the brave stand that all births are sacred, that there is no such thing as an illegitimate child. Even if you believe that some lives begin in sin, all sins should be forgiven. The single mother and her baby must be seen as a family and offered help to survive as a family, not punished for the "sin" of being a fatherless family, since fifty percent of today's youth will live in a single parent home before they are eighteen as a result of divorce.

Religious groups might do better to help stem the divorce rate through more family education at the high school and junior high school levels. Another constructive alternative would be if everyone who cherishes life took into their home one "unadoptable" child. Preventing the destruction of life

158

is a goal we all share. But who among us shall sit in judgment as to who is fit to parent that life and who is not?

SINGLE PARENTS need to continue to be recognized as capable parents regardless of age, education, race or economics. Government programs that were intended to offer temporary aid to those in need should be expanded, not removed. A mother and her baby are a basic family unit and deserve whatever support is required for them to stay together. More free and inexpensive housing needs to be made available for single parents. Fifty-five percent of American children have working mothers, yet America is the only advanced industrialized nation with no national maternity leave.

I agree with Ben J. Wattenberg, author of *The Birth Dearth*,[14] both in his concern for decreasing birth rates as well as in many of his suggested solutions. Wattenberg may well be an alarmist, but his primary suggestions: on-site day care centers in more U.S. firms, paid maternal leaves, flextime, job sharing, the re-establishment of the day-care tax credit, new day-care arrangements utilizing the skills of the elderly are all ideas worth trying. In addition to helping single mothers, they would, according to Wattenberg, help encourage married women not to defer childbirth for economic reasons which would therefore help decrease infertility.

Single parents who indicate a need to surrender their children to adoption should be required to be seen by an independent family counselor who, looking at single mothers and their children as newly emerging families in stress as well as part of an extended family, would help their clients to explore their motives and alternatives and to clearly spell out the outcomes of all alternatives, including surrender, just as a family counselor would do for a couple considering divorce, making no value judgments as to which alternative is "best." No final plans should be made prior to the birth and for *at least thirty,* preferably ninety days after. All mothers who are physically and mentally able to, should be encouraged to care for their children while long-term plans are being made, with emergency foster care being provided for mothers *and* their babies when necessary. Single new mothers need to be helped to see their feelings of inadequacy as natural.

Part of the duty of the family counselor assigned to the case would be to involve the extended family and/or father whenever possible. Unwed mothers often fear involving their families when in fact they may prove to be concerned and helpful. Counselors would work with their clients toward seeing their families and/or the child's father as possible resources which should not be overlooked and who have legal rights to the child. Fathers and other family members should always be offered the opportunity of keeping their related children before a stranger adoption is considered. Adoptive parents would only be sought after new mothers and their extended families have demonstrated beyond a reasonable doubt that they do not want their children despite all efforts to help them achieve family unity.

Mothers who express a determination to surrender their children after being informed of the life-long effects would then have to present their cases before a board consisting of their family counselor, a psychologist, a social worker, one or more adult adoptees, one or more birthparent. It would be the job of the board to see to it that the mothers have indeed been informed of their option to parent; made aware of resources and declined to utilize them; made aware of the long-term trauma surrendering children has been docu- mented to cause; the delayed grief they may suffer; the possibility of secondary infertility; and the possible effect that their ability to parent subsequent children may be im- paired as a result of surrendering. They would be made to sign a statement that they have been made aware of all of these facts.

TEMPORARY FOSTER CARE should no more be sug- gested to women considering adoption than it would be to any other who has given birth, married or not. Any separa- tion of mothers and their babies is potentially dangerous to the bonding process and can scar the emotional well-being of the growing child into adulthood, and therefore should be used most judicially, and only in cases where it is for the

160

physical safety of the child. If a new mother needs time to think and/or to make housing or employment arrangements, a home where she and her new baby can be together needs to be provided for this purpose.

BIRTHPARENTS should be permitted to select adoptive parents whose desire for ongoing openness would be most in keeping with their own. Birthparents should have the right to an attorney present at the time of relinquishment. The relinquishment of parenthood should not be an open-ended relinquishment to an agency, social system or other intermediary but directly to the adoptive parents of choice. Any desire for continued communication and/or visitation should be put into a written contract at the time of surrender or at any time thereafter. Every adoption should automatically contain a Right of First Refusal clause which specifies that the relinquishing parent will be notified by the agency in the event that the adoption is not finalized for any reason, or in the event the adoption is terminated for any reason. Since the original agreement was that the child be relinquished to the custody of the adopting couple, the birthparents should also be notified in the event of the death or divorce of the adoptive parent or parents which would leave the child with only one of the two designated parents, or where custody might be assigned to a relative of the original adopters. In each such case, the birthparents should retain the right to re-open a custody suit based on the current status of the adoptive home and the current status of the birthparents.

Family counseling should not end for birthparents upon relinquishment, but needs to continue to help them through the initial stages of grief and to suggest self-help groups which can follow-up at various stages as such help may be needed.

OPEN ADOPTION offers definite advantages not found in the closed and secret type of adoption. Originally it was believed to be best for adoptive parents to pretend it was their own child. Current adoption laws reflect the principle of secrecy to "protect" children from their illegitimate status. We are currently seeing the results of dishonesty on those whom it was intended to protect. There is no doubt that honesty and openness are more conducive to the mental wellness of children raised in adoptive families.

Open adoptions vary greatly, but in general the adopting couple and the birthparents "choose" one another, often through resumes and/or photos. Many meet to make certain of their choice and to finalize plans for the adoption. Ideally, both sets of parents are available to each other and to the children on an ongoing basis. Visitation may occur after the placement if this has been included in the agreement. Pictures, letters and vital information are often shared between the two sets of parents at pre-determined intervals and for a pre-determined length of time. Open adoption is not the same as using an agency or an attorney as a repository for the identifying information that is to be made available to the adoptee at the age of majority. What makes an adoption open is that identities are known and shared by birth and adoptive parents. Ideally the identity of the birthparent(s) would be an integral part of the growing adoptee's life.

All adoptions should be open adoptions; however, as an advocate of mothers and babies I view the current use of open adoption with caution. Just as anonymity was the major "selling point" of the sixties, openness in adoption is the key word of the eighties. Books such as *To Love and Let Go*[15] reflect a limited attitude that proclaims the wonders of such innovative open adoption arrangements. While openness and honesty are, of course, preferable to dishonesty and secrecy, one case, within Arms' book, ended with promises not kept to the birthmother. I have heard of many more such broken promises. Desperation for a child may lead some prospective adopters to initially agree to any condition in order to obtain a child, often with the intent of keeping promises made, only to find that they are unable or unwilling to continue to keep the lines of communication open. Caution needs to prevail in offering open adoption to expectant mothers who might mistakenly see open adoption as a way to have the best of both worlds. Even under the best of cir-

162

cumstances, birthparents have less rights than non-custodial parents in a divorce and this difference needs to be explained clearly. Open adoption offers birthparents the peace of knowing that their children are alive and well, but pictures and even visits cannot replace the lost parenting experience.

Those who do choose open adoption should do so through progressive agencies such as Lutheran Family Services of Houston, Texas, or Children's Home Society of California, which can assure that pre-adoption agreements are kept. Private arrangements are a great deal more risky to both parties for many reasons, including revocation of surrender, and are therefore not recommended. However, if one chooses such an arrangement it would be advisable to have all agreements notarized. It is important to realize that our court system is currently able to do very little to locate non-custodial parents who abduct their children and even less to locate fathers who are delinquent in child support payments. One can only guess how much time and expense, if any, a court would justify to locate adoptive parents who changed their names and moved to another state to avoid continued communications with birthparents who relinquished all legal custody.

If the preceding suggestions in regard to expectant mothers considering adoption were carried through, there should be little need for open adoption. If we eliminate family, social and financial pressure, *women either want their children or they do not.* If they want them, resources need to be found to offer them the support they and their children need to remain together. If they do not want their children, one would have to wonder why they would seek an open adoption. Ideally, adoption would only serve orphans whose parents have deceased or who are unable or unwilling to parent them and who have no extended family members who are able and willing to care for them. The circumstances surrounding their placement, however unpleasant, are their reality and their birthright. An institutionalized parent, or elderly grandparent are the adoptee's extended family and need to be embraced by the adoptive family as such, not feared.

OPEN RECORDS are not to be confused with open adoption. While open adoption is a possible solution for those who will be making adoption a part of their lives in the future, opening of the sealed adoption records would humanize adoption for those who have been oppressed by its antiquated regulations. Open records would allow adult adoptees the same access to their birth records any other adult citizen in this country has. Laura L. Valenti says of sealed adoption, "Under no other circumstances are non-criminals treated with so little regard for their personal freedom and decisions concerning their own lives."[16]

Sorosky, Baran and Pannor investigated the sealed record controversy in 1978 and came to the very firm conclusion that opening the records was the only humane and sensible solution. While many adoption professionals have since echoed their conclusions, little has been done to facilitate such a practice. In fact, the state of Pennsylvania took a step backward in 1985, sealing up a loophole in the law which allowed adult adoptees access to their original birth records. Meanwhile, during the late '80s adoption records were unsealed in New Zealand and parts of Canada.

Open records need not be feared. In England and other countries where the records are open, only about ten percent of all adopted persons avail themselves of the information. Those adoptive families in this country who have opened their hearts to embrace their childrens' biological families have found that it has brought them closer, not further apart.

Laura Valenti expresses the hope that "In the years ahead, open records will become a reality. It is a matter of time and equal rights."[17]

VOLUNTARY MUTUAL CONSENT REGISTRIES are being promoted and passed into law in many states such as Texas, New York and New Jersey as the perfect compromise solution. Only those adoptees and birthparents who wish to meet one another would register and be matched. Those who do not wish to have their identities known would remain anonymous. While this may sound ideal, and may be adequate for those pursuing a search out of curiosity and a

164

general interest, it is insufficient for the adopted person in need of medical history.

Many such state registries require the consent of the adult adoptees' adoptive parents. Is there anything else that you can think of which requires an American *adult* to obtain parental consent? This is insulting and perpetuates the myth that an adoptee remains forever a child and the chatteled possession of his adopters.

There are other problems as well. It is not uncommon for women to travel to distant cities to birth and surrender their children. Back home, years later, they may be unaware that such registries exist in the state in which their children were born. Adoptees who are not matched when paying their fee and placing their names in such a registery must reckon with the following possibilities: their mothers have not registered because they do not know that the registry exists, or they may be deceased. The adopted person may have siblings and other family members who would be more than willing to know him, but he is denied the opportunity, even to medical information, if his mother has not registered.

Registry restrictions are so numerous that registries in fact serve to hinder more reunions than they create.[18] The Michigan Adoption Registry, in the period from September, 1979 to February, 1983, had consents filed by 2,205 birthparents and 1,692 adopted adults wishing reunion. There were one hundred and three "matches."

American adults do not need such elaborate protections built into their personal relations, and have none in any other area of their lives. Are adult marriages arranged by matching only those who request to be matched, and who have their parents' consent? Do we need third party Cyrano de Bergerac intermediaries to announce our intentions to our beloveds? Suppose for a moment a woman entering into a marriage decided not to tell her husband about her previous lover. It would be her prerogative to lie. Now suppose her old flame came knocking on the door one day. She could refuse to see him and slam the door. If he persisted, she could obtain a restraining order. But the law could not prevent him from knowing her name and where she lived simply to pro-

165

tect her lie. Why then should laws be needed to protect any two adults from one another? Because birthparents were promised anonymity? Most did not ask for it, and few want it now. What of those who do wish to remain anonymous? They have the same right to say "I don't want to see you" and slam the door. They have the same right to obtain a restraining order in the rare instance that the person initiating the reunion would not take no for an answer.

The Oakland County Branch of the American Civil Liberties Union (Michigan) has adopted a policy of opposing sealed adoption records. The policy, which contends that present law discriminates against the civil liberties of adult adoptees, states in part, ". . . laws suppressing information about adoptees or their birthparents, laws allowing access to such information only upon court order, deny to adoptees, their birth parents, and their relatives the equal protection of the laws, and constitute an unwarranted interference by government with the right of people to choose whether to associate. The ACLU believes that all persons have a right to privacy. Adoptees, their birth parents and other relatives have no greater right to privacy than any other person." The Oakland County branch has recommended that the State ACLU adopt this policy and recommend it for national adoption. Likewise, the Southwest Florida Chapter of ACLU also favors open records and recommends it for Florida State policy.

ADOPTIVE PARENTS who have worked through their infertility and have separated their desire to have a parenting experience from all of the other aspects of childbearing that have been lost to them will make better adoptive parents than those who have not. Therefore, every prospective adoptive couple should be seen by a family counselor (just as each surrendering parent would be). Counselors would work with the couples in order to determine their feelings about their fertility and how far they have come in accepting the permanency of their loss and realizing that only parenting will be achieved through adoption. Counselors should see the couples, both together and individually, in order to determine if the level of acceptance, desire and motivation to adopt are mutual.

All adopters should be asked how they would feel about learning to love one of the many older, handicapped or non-white children who so desperately need homes. In addition to attempting to help find homes for homeless children, through such dialogue the counselor has the opportunity to observe the couples' attitude toward parenting. Couples should be counseled as to the prognostic outcome adoption may have on their marriage and should be questioned about how members of their extended family will accept their adopted children.

Most importantly, they need to be able to accept the fact that the children they adopt into their families have two sets of parents. The adopters will become the only psychological parents their children will ever know (even if there are visits from birthparents). It is of utmost importance for the psychological well-being of their children that they respect the children's origins as much as they respect and love their children, for one is an inseparable part of the other. They need to be able to speak about the birthparents with the same air one would speak of any distant relative, showing neither animosity nor insecurity.

ADOPTEES must have access to their original birth information the same as any other citizen. Certificates of adoption would indicate the adoptive parents' names and would be used for all legal purposes. Such certificates would state where the original birth records were recorded.

POST ADOPTIVE SERVICES need to be made available for all parties of the triangle: to help birthparents recognize the long-term effects of unresolvable grief; to help adoptees deal with their feelings of rejection; and to help adoptive parents through not just the difficult "telling" times, but to see adoption as an ongoing process. The way in which adoption and birthparents are discussed in the adoptive family are of the utmost importance in helping to establish a foundation of self-worth in the adopted person.

167

STATISTICS need to be gathered in areas where they are lacking in order to make more intelligent decisions about the future of adoption. Some areas that need verified statistics are: the number of out-of-family adoptions per year in this country; the number of foreign adoptions; the number of independent adoptions; the number of agency adoptions; the number of adoptive couples which divorce; the number of independent adoptions terminated after finalization; the number of agency adoptions terminated after finalization; the number of reported cases of abuse in adoptive families; secondary infertility and impaired parenting among birthparents.

RESEARCH projects which would be of help in the future of adoption could be funded by the National Institute of Mental Health, Washington, D.C., under the auspices of the Child Welfare League of America. A few suggested areas for future research include:

• Does the stress of adopting add to the divorce rate?

• The incest taboo and its effect on sexual abuse in adoptive families;

• Absence of kinship and its effect on abuse in adoptive homes;

• A comparative study of adopted persons in therapy and those coping without professional counseling with particular emphasis on how and when each group was told of his adoption;

• A longitudinal study of independent versus agency adoptions in terms of outcome, terminations, the effects on all parties;

• The long-term effect of surrendering on birthparents in terms of marriage, fertility, and ability to parent subsequent children;

• A longitudinal study of open versus closed adoption and its effect on all parties.

168

SOCIAL ATTITUDES need to be helped to positively sanction childless couples. As infertility increases and the supply of adoptable infants continues to dwindle, marriage without children needs to become a viable and socially acceptable alternative. This can be accomplished through government sponsored educational programs, just as the two child family was encouraged to become the "norm" during the forties.

Society needs to heighten its sensitivities regarding adoptees and adoption realizing that neither are a joke. Society needs to learn to know and understand birthparents.

Adoption has been compared to marriage in that people who are not biologically related learn to love and live together as a family. While this analogy is true to that limited extent, there are also many areas of difference. With marriage, because the parties are not biologically connected, the arrangement can be severed by divorce. In a marriage two consenting adults agree to the arrangement, in adoption the party being "chosen" is a minor who takes no part in the decision. In a marriage ties are not cut with the family of origin, in traditional adoption they have been. For birthparents, particularly, adoption more closely resembles a divorce than a marriage, for while parents are said to "lose" their children to marriage, they are losing grown children with whom they have shared lifetimes of memories. While there is a certain sadness to that type of loss, there are also tears of joy and a future of grandchildren to look forward to. Mothers who lose children to adoption, lose their children's childhood and that of their grandchildren as well. Adoptees lose all connectedness with their heredity and past. The marriage analogy, while not true today, is perhaps a goal worth striving toward. Adoptees could maintain a loving respect for their families of birth while being psychologically and lovingly bonded to their nurturing family.

Adoption can and should be a happy "marriage" of orphaned children and loving families, but our social system dictates that minor children not be removed from their families of origin without good cause. Adoption which involves taking as well as giving, loss as well as gain, and a legal alteration of nature's plan, should be handled with utmost caution, respect and professionalism. That current adoption is not working optimally has been clearly demonstrated. However, change, too, must be looked at cautiously and from the perspective of the impact on all three parties. If the impact is traumatic and/or long-lasting on any one of the parties, as it is now, adoption cannot be viewed as positive.

Only when all of these goals have been accomplished can we consider adoption to be truly humane. Rather than a triangle with sharp angles, dagger-like points and sides which often try not to meet, when everyone involved in adoption puts the needs of the adoptees foremost and central, and when all those who care about children join hands to work together toward the mutual goal of humanizing adoption, the adoption triangle can be softened into a circle of love, respect and mutual understanding. The center of the circle—and the center of everyone's concern—being adopted persons.

Appendix of Organizations

Inclusion of a group or organization in this listing is not an endorsement. Hundreds of search and support groups exist throughout the country and it would be impossible to list them all. When writing to a group for information, the more information you supply, the better able they will be to help you or to refer you to the best place for help. State whether you are an adoptee, birthparent, etc. State where and when the birth and adoption took place. Always include a self-addressed, stamped business-size envelope for a reply.

AAC—American Adoption Congress, P.O. Box 44040, L'Enfant Plaza Station, Washington, D.C. 20026-0040

Adoption Circle, 401 East 74th Street, Suite 17D, New York, NY 10021

Adoption Connection, Inc., 11 Peabody Square, Room #1, Peabody, MA 01960

Adoption Forum, 6808 Ridge Ave. (rear), Philadelphia, PA 19128

AIE—Adoption Information Exchange, P.O. Box 4153, Chapel Hill, NC 27515-4153

ALARM—Adopting Legislation for Adoption Reform Movement, P.O. Box 2391, Ft. Myers, FL 33902

AIM—Adoption Identity Movement, 1434 Southland Dr., S.W., Grand Rapids, MI 49509

ALMA—Adoptees' Liberty Movement Association, Box 154 Washington Bridge Station, New York, NY 10033* **

Angles & Extensions, 1850 Azaela Springs Trail, Roswell, GA 30075

APFOR—Adoptive Parents for Open Records, Inc., P.O. Box 193, Long Valley, NJ 07853

ASK—Adoptees Search for Knowledge, 8107 Webster Road, Mt. Morris, MI 48458

BSN—The Birthparent Support Network, P.O. Box 120, No. White Plains, NY 10603

Caring Hearts, P.O. Box 36111, Decatur, GA 30032-0111

CUB—Concerned United Birthparents, 2000 Walker Street, Des Moines, IA 50317* **

Heritage Inc., Box 84524, Las Vegas, NV 89185

ISSR—International Soundex Reunion Registry, P.O. Box 2312, Carson City, NV 89702-2312**

Jigsaw, GPO Box 526 BB, Melbourne 3001, Australia

ORA—Oregon Adoption Rights, Box 1332, Beaverton, OR 97075

OASIS—Organized Adoption Search Information Services, Box 53761, Miami Shores, FL 33153

Operation Identity, 13101 Blackstone NE, Albuquerque, NM 87111

172

ORIGINS, P.O. Box 444, East Brunswick, NJ 08816

Orphan Voyage, 2141 Road 2300, Cedaredge, CO 81413

PACER—Post Adoption Center for Education & Research, 2255 Ignacio Valley Rd., Suite L, Walnut Creek, CA 94598

Parent Finders, 1408 W. 45th Ave., Vancouver, B.C. V6M 2H1* **

Roots and Reunions, P.O. Box 121, L'Anse, MI 49946

Searchline, 1516 Old Orchard, Irving, TX 75061

Ties That Bind, P.O. Box 3119, Milford, CT 06460

TriAdoption Library, Inc., P.O. Box 638, Westminster, CA 92684

Truth Seekers in Adoption, P.O. Box 366, Prospect Heights, IL 60070-0366

WARM—Washington Adoptees' Rights Movement, 15749 NE 4th Room 12, Bellevue, WA 98008

Wichita Adult Adoptees, 5402 Polo, Wichita, KS 67208

---

*National Headquarters—many branches.
**Registry.

Notes

INTRODUCTION

1. (New York: New American Library, 1981).
2. 669 Airport Freeway, Suite 310, Hurst, TX 76053.
3. P.O. Box 277, New Paltz, NY 12561.
4. (New York: Simon & Schuster, 1986).
5. ". . . A Name You Never Got." Baby Bunny Productions, Oakland, CA 94618.
6. (New York: Viking Press, 1987).
7. Frederick H. Stone, "Adoption and Identity," Royal Hospital for Sick Children, *Child Psychiatry & Human Development,* Glasgow, Scotland, 2 (Spring, 1972) p. 30.

CHAPTER ONE
DISPELLING THE MYTHS

1. (New York: Harper & Row, 1984).
2. David H. Kirk, *Adoptive Kinship: A Modern Institution in Need of Reform* (Canada: Butterworth, 1981), p. 4.
3. "What's Right—And What's Wrong—About Adoption Today," *Redbook,* September, 1978, p. 39.
4. Claudia Wallis, "The New Origins of Life," *Time,* 10 September, 1984, pp. 46-53.
5. HBO Pictures.
6. 10845 Vanowen St., N. Hollywood, CA 91605.

7. Style number 95 0130, California Dreamers, Chicago 60610.
8. "What's Right," p. 42.
9. (New York: Free Press of Glencoe, 1964).
10. (Toronto: Butterworth, 1981).
11. New York: Paddington, 1977.
12. The Center for Adoptive Families, New York.
13. Mary Kathleen Benet, *The Politics of Adoption* (New York: Free Press, 1976), p. 186.
14. Arthur D. Sorosky, Annette Baran and Reuben Pannor, *The Adoption Triangle: The Effects of the Sealed Record on Adoptees, Birthparents and Adoptive Parents* (New York: Anchor/Doubleday, 1979), p. 37.
15. Lynn Giddens, *Faces of Adoption* (Chapel Hill, NC: Amberly Publications, 1983), p. 51.

CHAPTER TWO
ADOPTEES: A POPULATION AT RISK

1. (New York: W.W. Norton, 1953), p. 92.
2. Carin Rubenstein, "An Evolutionary Basis for Step-parents' Neglect?" *Psychology Today,* December, 1980, p. 31.
3. Joan M. Jones and R.L. McNeely, "Mothers Who Neglect and Those Who Do Not: A Comparative Study," *Social Casework: The Journal of Contemporary Social Work* (November, 1980): pp. 559-67.
4. Jill Krementz, *How It Feels to Be Adopted* (New York: Knopf, 1982).
5. "More and More Adoptions Now End in Failure," *The Bergen* (New Jersey) *Record,* 18 March, 1984, p. A-1.
6. WNYW-FOX-TV.
7. LACASA Open Record, October/November, 1984 and ALMA Chirstmas Album, 1984.
8. "The 'Throwaway' Children," *Newsday,* 18 November, 1984, p. 4.
9. "A Comparison of Self-Concept in Adopted and Non-Adopted Adolescents," *Adolescence,* Vol. XII, No. 47 (Fall, 1977): pp. 443-8.
10. "Pioneer for Adoption Reform," *Exchange: An Adoption Research Project* (1984) Vol. 2, No. 4.
11. *Twice Born* (New York: Dial Press, 1979), *Lost and*

Found (New York: Dial Press, 1979), *I'm Still Me* (New York: Knopf, 1981).
12. "Adult Adoptees as Children Pressing Hunt for Parents," *New York Times,* 13 July, 1980, p. XI, 2:1.
13. S. Farber, "Sex Differences in the Expression of Adoption Ideas: Observations of Adoptees from Birth-Latency," *American Journal of Orthopsychiatry,* 47(4) (October, 1974).
14. Truth Seekers in Adoption newsletter, 1983.
15. Roberta Ostroff, "Growing Up Behind Locked Doors," *Rolling Stone,* 20 November, 1986, p. 76.
16. M. Bohman and Al Von Knorring, "Psychiatric Illness Among Adults Adopted as Infants," *Acta Psyciatri Scand,* 60(1) (July, 1979).
17. Mary J. Blotcky, John G. Looney & Keith D. Grace, "Treatment of the Adopted Adolescent: Involvement of the Biological Mother," *Journal of the American Academy of Child Psychiatry,* 21 (1982), 3, p. 281.
18. John Triseliotis, *In Search of Origins: The Experience of Adopted People* (Boston: Beacon Press, 1973), p. 7.
19. Margaret Kornitzer, "Adoption and Family Life."
20. (New York: Simon & Shuster, 1983).
21. (New York: The Free Press, 1983).
22. "How Adoption System Ignites a Fire," *New York Times,* 1 March, 1983, p. 27.
23. New York: Plenum Press, 1985.
24. (San Antonio, Texas: Corona, 1982).
25. "Open Adoption: The Reasons, the Risks," *McCall's,* September, 1987, p. 137.

CHAPTER THREE
BIRTHPARENTS: UNRESOLVABLE GRIEF

1. See Appendix of Organizations.
2. *The Adoption Triangle,* p. 27.
3. Ibid, p. 37.
4. *Let's Talk About Adoption* (Toronto: Little Brown), p. 184.
5. *Death by Adoption* (New Zealand: Cicada Press, 1979), p. 7.
6. The Willows Nursery, a private non-sectarian institution

in Kansas City, Missouri, which placed approximately 35,000 children between 1905 and 1969.

7. (Trumansburg, New York: Crossing Press).
8. "Death by Adoption: Symbolic Murder," *Origins*, January/February, 1984.
9. *Faces of Adoption*, p. 59.
10. Statement of Joan Gasper, Deputy Assistant Secretary for Population Affairs before the Congressional Coalition on Adoption, 17 April, 1986.
11. The Quality of Life, Golden Cradle, 555 East City Avenue, Bala Cynwyd, PA 19004.
12. "Why Are People Mad at Mr. Stork?" 21 August, 1983, p. 17.
13. Eva Y. Deykin, Lee Campbell and Patricia Patti, "The Postadoption Experience of Surrendering Parents," *American Journal of Orthopsychiatry*, 54(2) (April, 1984): pp. 27.
14. *Death by Adoption*, p. 8.
15. "Orientation of Pregnancy Counselors Toward Adoption," prepared under Grant #APR 000902 by Edmund Mech at the University of Illinois and submitted to the Office of Adolescent Pregnancy Programs, Department of Health and Human Services.
16. Bernard Gavzer, "Who Am I?" *Parade*, 27 October, 1985.
17. Doris H. Bertucci, "On Adoption," *Social Work: the Journal of the National Association of Social Workers* (May, 1987): Vol. 23, No. 3.
18. Legislative Research Commission—"Rights of Adopted Children" report to the 1981 General Assembly of North Carolina.
19. Memorandum, 21 November, 1980, Director of North Carolina Division of Social Services entitled "Presentation for Public Hearing on Rights of Adopted Children," Robin Peacock, Legislative Research Commission, p. 8.
20. Kate Weinstein, "Mothers In Exile: The Aftermath of Surrendering a Baby for Adoption," *Feeling Great* (New York: Haymarket Group) No. 13, July, 1985, p. 66.
21. Delores Schmidt, "Dual Heritage: The Challenge of Adoption," *Charities USA*, March, 1980, p. 9.
22. "Mothers In Exile," p. 66.

23. *Faces of Adoption,* p. 60.
24. Edward K. Rynearson, "Relinquishment and Its Maternal Complications: A Preliminary Study," *American Journal of Psychiatry,* 139:3 (March, 1982): pp. 339.
25. *Faces of Adoption,* p. 83.
26. Deykin et al, p. 276-7.
27. (MA: Bergin & Garvey, 1984).
28. Extracted from "Shadows of Ourselves," *Origins,* May/June, 1986.
29. Originally published as "Adoption Agony," *Origins,* March/April, 1983.
30. See Appendix of Organizations.
31. Ibid.
32. *Origins,* May/June, 1986.
33. *Mothering,* P.O. Box 1960, Santa Fe, NM 87504.
34. *Origins,* May/June, 1984.
35. "Mothers In Exile," p. 67.
36. "Opt to Adopt," *Womanity,* 2141 Youngs Valley Rd., Walnut Creek, CA 94596.

CHAPTER FOUR
ADOPTIVE PARENTING:
OVERCOMING THE OBSTACLES

1. *The Little Victims: How America Treats Its Children* (New York: McKay, 1975), p. 8.
2. *Adoptalk,* a publication of the North American Council on Adoptable Children, July/August, 1983.
3. *OURS,* March/April, 1981, p. 15.
4. Ibid, p. 16.
5. (Boston: Beacon Press, 1973), p. xi.
6. "Center Helps Parents Adapt to Adoption," *New York Daily News,* 2 March, 1984.
7. Public Hearing before Assembly Institutions, Health & Welfare on Assembly Bill No. 2051 (Adoption), 9 December, 1981, Trenton, NJ.
8. "A Comparison of Self-Concept in Adopted and Non-Adopted Adolescents," *Adolescence* (Fall, 1977) Vol. XII, No. 47, p. 447.
9. Bernard Asbell, "Why So Many Adoptions Fail," *Good Housekeeping,* August, 1962, p. 166.

10. "Adoption and Disrupted Narcissism: A Case Illustration of a Latency Boy," p. 487.
11. "Parenting and Parentage: Distinct Aspects of Children's Importance," *Family Relations,* January, 1983.
12. Diane M. Zwimpfer, "Indicators of Adoption Breakdown," Social Casework: *The Journal of Contemporary Social Work* (March 1983): pp. 169-177.
13. Presentation before the American Adoption Congress, panel on Physical and Emotional Needs in Adoption, Washington, D.C., 5 May, 1979.
14. *Let's Talk About Adoption* (Toronto: Little, Brown), p. 93.
15. *In Search of Origins,* pp. 155-6.
16. Disturbed Narcissism, p. 487.
17. Claire Berman, "Raising an Adopted Child," Public Affairs Pamphlet No. 620, p. 8.
18. "Why So Many Adoptions Fail," p. 167.
19. *The Fifteen Most Asked Questions About Adoption* (Scottsdale, PA: Herald Press, 1985), p. 177.
20. Constance Hoenk Shapiro & Betsy Crane Seeber, "Sex Education and the Adoptive Family," *Social Work* (July/August, 1983), p. 291.
21. "Pioneer for Adoption Reform," *Exchange.*
22. Outlook, the newsletter for the Department of Psychiatry of New York: Cornell Medical Center, Winter, 1985.
23. *Let's Talk About Adoption,* p. 91.
24. Ibid.
25. Lost & Found newsletter, Ohio, July, 1984.
26. (New York: Avon Books, 1979), p. 38.
27. North East Ohio *Lost and Found,* July, 1984.
28. Page 38.

CHAPTER FIVE
THE RIGHT OF FIRST REFUSAL

1. Based on a personal interview.
2. Ibid.
3. Laurie Wishard & William Wishard, *Adoption: The Grafted Tree* (New York: Avon Books, 1979), p. 78.
4. Based on a personal interview.

5. Adapted from CUB *Communicator,* February, 1982, p. 3.
6. *People,* 2 March, 1987, p. 29-31.

CHAPTER SIX
ADOPTION: A CIRCLE OF LOVE

1. Marsha Riben, "Adoption: A Circle of Love," *Mothering,* Winter, 1983.
2. "What's Right," p. 39.
3. Wendy Smith, "Baby Farm," *Time,* 4 August, 1986, p. 40.
4. Peggy Mann, "New Help for the Childless," *Reader's Digest,* January, 1986, p. 139.
5. "It's the No. 1 Venereal Disease in America," *People,* 15 April, 1985, p. 139.
6. Ben Wattenberg, *The Birth Dearth* (New York: Pharos Books, 1987).
7. "Big Demand, Tight Supply."
8. (New York: Harper & Row, 1986).
9. *Newsweek,* 14 January, 1985.
10. "Why Teenage Pregnancy Rates are Rising in the U.S.," *Parade,* 25 September, 1985.
11. "Teenage Parenthood and Economic Dependence," *Social Work* (January/February, 1984).
12. "Do Americans Hate Children?" *Ms.,* November, 1983, p. 127, excerpted from Progrebin, *Family Politics* (New York: McGraw Hill, 1984), p. 127.
13. *The Tender Gift* (New York: Schocken, 1976).
14. New York: Paddington, 1977.
15. (New York: Knopf, 1983).
16. *The Fifteen Most Asked Questions*
17. Ibid.
18. David H. Kirk, Adoptive Kinship: A Modern Institution in Need of Reform (Toronto: Butterworth, 1981), p. 136.

Glossary of Terms

ADOPTED CHILD—A baby or a child who was born to one set of parents and raised by another through the legal relinquishment of parental rights by the parents of birth. It is incorrect to use this term to describe an adult who was adopted as a child.

ADOPTEE—An adopted person of any age who is herein referred to with a masculine pronoun, unless referring to a specific female adoptee.

ADOPTERS—See adoptive parents.

ADOPTION—Unless otherwise stated, this term refers to non-relative adoption, as opposed to step-parent adoption or adoption within the extended family. In almost all cases, adoption herein refers to the placement of infants as opposed to older children or children with "special needs."

ADOPTIVE PARENTS—Unless otherwise stated, this term refers to infertile couples as opposed to "preferential adopters," those who choose to adopt despite and/or in addition to their ability to bear children.

AGENCY—Licensed private, state or religious organizations which are authorized by law to act as intermediaries between birth and adoptive parents.

AMENDED CERTIFICATE—An altered certificate of birth issued at the time an adoption is finalized. This certificate falsely states that the child was born to the adoptive parents and in no way indicates the word adoption. This is the only certificate an adopted person of any age has access to in most states.

BIOLOGICAL MOTHER—A term which is being replaced by birthmother because of its clinical coldness.

BIRTHPARENT—Currently the most widely accepted term for the mother and/or father of a child who is subsequently surrendered to adoption.* **

COOPERATIVE ADOPTION—See open adoption.

INDEPENDENT ADOPTION—Another term for private adoption.

MUTUAL CONSENT REGISTRIES—Voluntary cross-reference indexes, generally state run, which, for a fee, keep adoptees' birth information on file and match it with birthparents who likewise register. Most have age restrictions and many require the consent of the adult adoptees' adoptive parents.

NATURAL MOTHER—This term is fading from use because it was found to be offensive to adoptive parents who claim that use of the word "natural" to describe the

---

*Much of the birthparent chapter is written from a female perspective as the childbearer, with the role of the birthfather described more briefly. While there are exceptions, birthfathers generally do not take as active a role in the pregnancy, the adoption plan, the surrender and the unresolvable grief as do birthmothers. Those birthfathers who do mourn the loss of their parenting role can relate to what is written about birthmothers because it will apply equally to them.
**I personally prefer the term original mother(s) and original parent(s) because they more aptly define a child's first parents. I feel that the terms birthmother(s) and birthparent(s) attempt to limit our role to one day in the life of our children. I have used the latter, however, because they have become more widely used and accepted.

184

woman who bore the child they parent, implies that adoptive parents are "unnatural."

OPEN ADOPTION—This term refers to adoptions in which there is knowledge of and communication between birth and adoptive families before and after placement. Also called cooperative adoption.

OPEN RECORDS—Legislation which would give adoptees access to their original birth and medical records just as any non-adopted citizen has.

PRIVATE ADOPTION—Adoptions arranged between adoptive and birthparents without an agency intermediary, often with an attorney and/or doctor intermediary. Legality varies state to state. Also called independent adoption.

RELINQUISH—To have your rights as a parent of your child terminated.

SURRENDER—See relinquish.

SEALED RECORDS—All information pertaining to the birth of a child who is subsequently surrendered for adoption. In most states the original certificates of birth are placed in "sealed" files which are accessible only to agency and vital statistic clerks, but not to the adoptee, adoptive parents or birthparents.

Suggested Reading

This is not a bibliography of books and articles used in the preparation of this book, nor is it intended to be an all-encompassing list of every book on the subject of adoption. It is merely a suggested reading list. Included are some books (i.e. *Sequencing, The Mother Machine, Mothers on Trial*) which are not direcly related to adoption but which impact on related subjects (i.e. parenting, reproductive technologies, custody). The inclusion of a book or article does not necessarily imply endorsement.

Allen, Elizabeth Cooper. *Mother, Can You Hear Me?* New York: Dodd, Meade & Co., 1983.

Ashkin, Jane. *Search: A Handbook for Adoptees and Birthparents.* New York: Harper & Row, 1982.

Baker, Nancy C. *Baby Selling: The Scandal of Black Market Adoption.* New York: Vanguard, 1987.

Benet, Mary Kathleen. *The Politics of Adoption.* New York: The Free Press, 1976.

Burgess, Linda. *The Art of Adoption.* Washington, D.C.: Acropolis, 1977.

Chesler, Phillis. *Mothers on Trial: The Battle for Children & Custody.* New York: McGraw Hill, 1985.

Corea, Gena. *The Mother Machine.* New York: Harper & Row, 1986.

Churchill, Sallie R. *No Child is Unadoptable: A Reader on Adoption of Children with Special Needs.* Beverly Hills, CA: Sage, 1979.

Corodoza, Arlene Rosen. *Sequencing: How to Have It All But Not All at Once.* New York: Atheneum, 1986.

Deykin, Eva Y.; Campbell, Lee and Patti Patricia. "The Postadoption Experience of Surrendering Parents." *American Journal of Orthopsychiatry,* 54(2), April, 1984, pp. 271-280.

Dusky, Lorraine, *Birthmark.* New York: Evans, 1979.

Erlich, Henry. *A Time to Search.* New York: Paddington, 1977.

Fisher, Florence. *The Search for Anna Fisher.* New York: Arthur Fields, 1973.

Giddens, Lynn. *Faces of Adoption.* Chapel Hill, NC: Amberly Publications, 1983.

Gilman, Lois. *The Adoption Resource Book.* New York: Harper & Row, 1984.

Hoffman, Alice. *Fortune's Daughter.* New York: G.P. Putnam, 1985.

Ingalls, Kate. *Living Mistakes: Mothers Who Consented to Adoption.* Winchester, MA: Allen Unwin, 1984.

James, Howard. *The Little Victims: How America Treats Its Children.* New York: David McKay, 1975.

Kirk, David H. *Adoptive Kinship: A Modern Institution in Need of Reform.* Canada: Butterworth & Co., 1981.

_____. *Shared Fate.* New York: Free Press of Glencoe, 1964.

Klibanoff, Elton and Susan. *Let's Talk About Adoption.* Boston: Little, Brown & Co., 1973.

Krementz, Jill. *How It Feels to be Adopted.* New York: Knopf, 1982.

Lifton, Betty Jean. *I'm Still Me.* New York: Knopf, 1981.

_____. *Lost and Found.* New York: Dial Press, 1979.

_____. *Twice Born: Memoirs of an Adopted Daughter.* New York: Dial Press, 1979.

Lindeman, Bard. *The Twins Who Found Each Other.* New York: Wm. Morrow, 1969.

Lowry, Lois. *Find a Stranger Say Goodbye.* Boston: Houghton Mifflin, 1978.

Maxtone-Graham, Katrina. *An Adopted Woman.* New York: Remi Books, 1980.

Millan, Leverett and Roll, Samuel. "Solomon's Mothers: A Special Case of Pathological Bereavement." *American Journal of Orthopsychiatry,* 55(3), July, 1985, pp. 411-18.

Musser, Sandra. *I Would Have Searched Forever.* Bala Cynwyd, PA: Jan Enterprises, 1979.

_____. *What Kind of Love Is This.* Oaklyn, NJ: Jan Publications, 1982.

Niles, Reg. *Reg Niles Searchbook.* Garden City, NY: Phileas Deigh Corp.

Riben, Marsha. "Adoption: A Circle of Love." *Mothering,* Winter, 1983.

_____. "Adoption May Not be the Best Option." New Jersey: *Suburban Parent,* May, 1987.

_____. "Jews and Adoption." Brooklyn, NY: *The Jewish Press,* January, 1987.

_____. "Coping with the Heartbreak of Losing a Child to Adoption." New Jersey: *Jersey Woman,* April, 1987.

_____. "The Sealed Record Controversy." New Jersey: *The Woman's Newspaper of Princeton,* May, 1983, pp. 12-13.

Rillera, Mary Jo. *Adoption Searchbook.* Westminster, CA: Triadoptions.

_____. *Adoption Encounter.* Westminster, CA: Triadoptions, 1987.

Rynearson, Edward K. "Relinquishment and Its Maternal Complications: A Preliminary Study." *American Journal of Psychiatry,* March, 1982, 139:3, pp. 338-40.

Shawyer, Joss. *Death by Adoption.* New Zealand: Cicada Press, 1979.

Silber, Kathleen and Speedlin, Phylis. *Dear Birthmother.* New York: Corona, 1983.

Sorosky, Arthur D.; Baron, Annette and Pannor, Reuben. *The Adoption Triangle.* New York: Doubleday/Anchor Press, 1979.

Triseltiotis, John. *In Search of Origins: The Experience of Adopted People.* Boston: Beacon Press, 1973.

Valenti, Laura L. *The Fifteen Most Asked Questions About Adoption.*

Wallenberg, Ben. *The Birth Dearth.* New York: Pharos Books, 1987.

Weinstein, Kate. "Mothers In Exile." *Feeling Great,* New York: Haymarket Group, No. 13, July, 1985, p. 65-8.

Wishard, Laurie and William. *Adoption: The Grafted Tree.* New York: Hearst, 1979.